English Code 4

Activity Book

Contents

OUR WORLD

INTRO:

Here we stand: children of every age,
This is our world and the world's our stage.
We can laugh, we can cry — we can float, we can fly,
We can dance, we can sing — we can do almost anything
in OUR world ... our *beautiful* world.

VERSE 1:

Some of us are small; some of us are tall,
Some of us are shy; some say hi to everybody,
Some of us like numbers; some of us love words,
Some of us watch football, and some of us watch the birds!

(CHORUS)

This is *our* world ... we're different but the same.
We live and learn together — we get to know each other ...
in OUR world ... our *beautiful* world.

VERSE 2:

Some of us like music; some of us like cars,
Some of us draw pictures, looking at the stars,
Some of us are scientists, trying to find the code,
All of us can help a friend and give a hand to hold.

This is *our* world — there's room for everyone.
We learn to live together, and we have a lot of fun ...
In ***our*** world ... in ***our*** world ... in our beautiful world!

Progress Chart

Unit 8

Unit 7

Unit 6

Unit 5

Unit 4

Unit 3

Unit 2

Unit 1

Creativity

Collaboration

Critical Thinking

Coding

Communication

Welcome back!

How can I talk about myself?

1  **Listen and write *Samir* or *Yuyan*.**

1 stayed in the city   _____

2 saw a lot of films   _____

3 visited some friends   _____

4 went to the park   _____

5 visited my family   _____

6 went to the beach   _____

7 went swimming   _____

8 went to the mountains   _____

Samir

2 **Write about your holiday.**

First, I _____ every day.

Then I _____ . I didn't _____ .

I saw _____ . I visited _____ .

Yuyan

3 **Choose an expression. Then ask and answer with a partner.**

> Give me five!   Here we are again!   Hey there!
> It's nice to see you.   What's new?   What's up?

Hey there! Where did you go on holiday?

I went to the beach.

4 **Describe a favourite holiday place.**

1 Where is it? My favourite holiday place is _____ .

2 When did you go there? I went _____ .

3 Who did you go with? _____

4 What did you do? _____

Big families

VOCABULARY

I will learn family words.

1 Make a family tree.

🍃 Find pictures of three generations in your family.

🍃 Copy the tree onto a large piece of paper.

🍃 Glue your picture to the top of the trunk.

🍃 Glue the other pictures to the branches around you.

2 Complete the information about your family.

My name: _____

Names of parents: _____

Names of grandparents: _____

_____

Number of brothers: _____   Number of sisters: _____

Number of uncles: _____   Number of aunts: _____

Number of cousins: _____   Number of others: _____

3 Read and complete.

1 My mum's mum is my _____ .   2 My mum's brother is my _____ .

3 My mum's dad is my _____ .   4 My cousin's mum is my _____ .

5 My aunt's child is my _____ .   6 My uncle's sister is my _____ .

7 My aunt's brother is my _____ .

4 Find out about a partner's family. Take notes.

Where are your grandparents from?

My grandparents are from Oaxaca.

Diego's grandparents are from Oaxaca.

Language lab

GRAMMAR: WHEN ...?

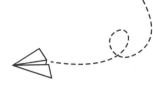
I will learn to ask and answer about dates.

1 🎧 003 Listen and write the dates.

Ismail's birthday:
_____ April

His mum's birthday:
_____ September

His dad's birthday:
_____ December

Ismail

His grandad's birthday: _____ October

His grandma's birthday: _____

Aunt Kate's birthday:

_____

Uncle Bob's birthday:

_____

Maryam's birthday:

_____

2 Look at 1. Write the dates in order. Use words.

1 _____   2 _____   3 _____

4 _____   5 _____   6 _____

7 _____   8 _____

3 Read and answer.

1 What's the date today?   _____

2 What's the date on Saturday?   _____

3 When is your birthday?   _____

4 When is your mum's birthday?   _____

4 ✏️ Make a birthday notebook.

* Attach 12 pieces of colourful paper together.

* Write the name of the months at the top of each piece of paper.

* Ask your friends and family about their birthdays and make a note of the dates.

* Write the dates in order and the person's name next to the date.

* Decorate the birthday notebook.

I can ask and answer about dates.

Story lab

READING

I will read a story about a birthday.

The **birthday** party

1 Read and circle T (True) or F (False).

1   The children think 70 is a special birthday.   T / F
2   Grandad thinks his birthday is special.   T / F
3   Mum doesn't want a party for Grandad.   T / F
4   The children invite their cousins.   T / F

2 Find words in the story that mean …

1   … had different ideas.   _____   2   … ask people to a party.   _____

3   … decoration for a cake.   _____   4   … a light for outside.   _____

5   … a surprise full of sweets.   _____   6   … didn't understand.   _____

3 Read and complete.

MATHS ZONE

Most years have got 365 days and February's got 28 days. But every four years, February's got 29 days and there are 366 days in the year. This is called a leap year. Grandad says he is _____ .   Grandad is really 17 x _____ = _____ .

4 Write your opinion of the story.

* Do you like Sofia and Samir? Why?
* What do you think is good about the birthday party?
* What do you think of the story?

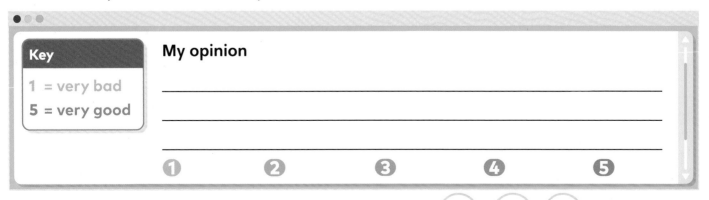

Key	**My opinion**
1 = very bad	
5 = very good	

①   ②   ③   ④   ⑤

I can   read a story about a birthday.

1 Into the wild

How can we plan a class adventure?

1 Read and complete.

branches grass leaves rocks trees

In the wild, we can collect 1 _____ ☐,
2 _____ ☐ and 3 _____ ☐.
We can climb 4 _____ ☐ and
5 _____ ☐. We can balance on
6 _____ ☐ and 7 _____ ☐.

2 004 Listen and tick ☑ the activities in 1.

3 Read and tick ☑ or cross ☒. Then answer.

Rose doesn't like climbing rocks. She likes climbing trees.

Tim doesn't like climbing trees or balancing on branches.

Anna likes climbing trees.

Dan likes climbing trees, but he doesn't like balancing on branches.

The girls like balancing on branches.

The boys like collecting leaves.

Each child likes two activities and doesn't like two activities.

CODE CRACKER

	Rose	Tim	Anna	Dan
climbing trees				
climbing rocks				
balancing on branches				
collecting leaves				

What is their favourite activity? _____

Values Look after the environment.

4 How can you look after wild spaces? Discuss with a partner.

You can look after wild spaces by taking your rubbish home.

In the forest

I will learn outdoor activity words.

VOCABULARY

1 Complete the crossword. Find the hidden words.

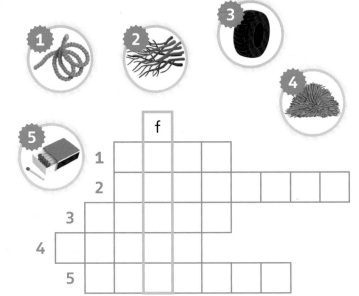

The hidden words are
_____ and _____ .

2 Write a new verse.

I said clap, clap, clap! I said stamp, stamp, stamp! I said let's get ready for adventure camp!

We've got _____ and _____ .

We've got _____ and _____ .

We've got _____ and _____ .

I said clap, clap, clap! I said stamp, stamp, stamp! I said let's get ready for adventure camp!

EXTRA VOCABULARY

3 🎧 005 Listen and label.

bottle   saucepan   tent   towel

1 _____   2 _____

_____   _____

4 **Ph** Look and match.

1 b_____d   2 l_____n   3 p_____ple

ur   ear   ir

Language lab

GRAMMAR: *GOING TO ...*

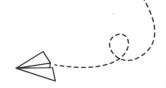

I will learn to talk about future plans using **going to**.

1 Follow the maze and tick ✓ the correct sentences.

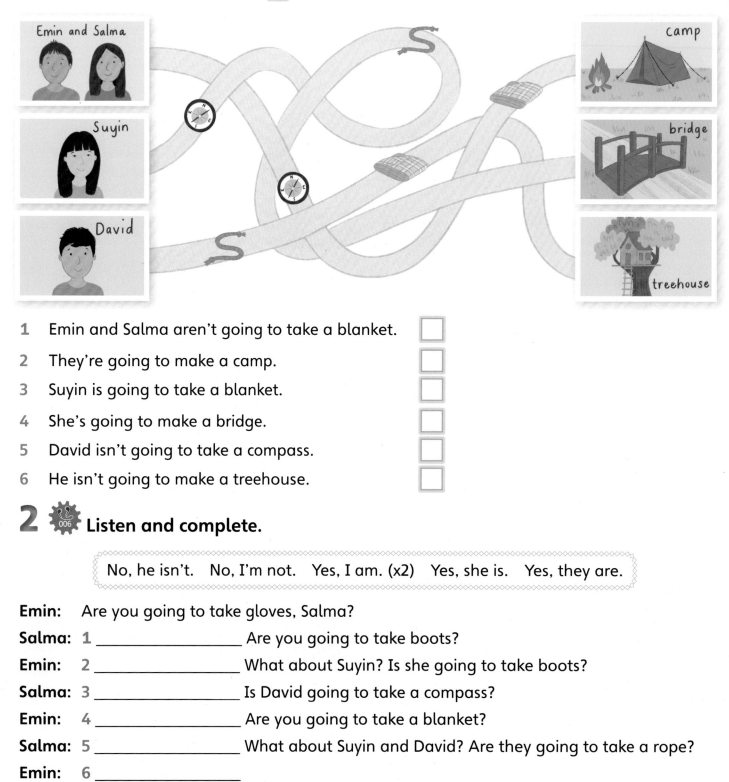

1   Emin and Salma aren't going to take a blanket. ☐

2   They're going to make a camp. ☐

3   Suyin is going to take a blanket. ☐

4   She's going to make a bridge. ☐

5   David isn't going to take a compass. ☐

6   He isn't going to make a treehouse. ☐

2 🎧 006 **Listen and complete.**

> No, he isn't.   No, I'm not.   Yes, I am. (x2)   Yes, she is.   Yes, they are.

Emin: Are you going to take gloves, Salma?

Salma: 1 _____ Are you going to take boots?

Emin: 2 _____ What about Suyin? Is she going to take boots?

Salma: 3 _____ Is David going to take a compass?

Emin: 4 _____ Are you going to take a blanket?

Salma: 5 _____ What about Suyin and David? Are they going to take a rope?

Emin: 6 _____

3 Whose list is it? Choose and complete.

David   Emin
Salma   Suyin

are going to make   aren't going to need
is going to make   is going to need
isn't going to need   isn't going to make

_____

○	boots
○	rope
○	gloves
○	compass

I think it is _____'s list. _____ _____
a bridge and _____ _____ boots.
_____ _____ a blanket because _____
_____ a camp.
It isn't Salma or Emin's list. They _____ a camp.
They _____ boots.

4 Choose a list and tick ☐.

☐ _____
blanket
whistle
compass
boots

☐ _____
boots
compass
rope
gloves

☐ _____
gloves
map
whistle
blanket

☐ _____
gloves
rope
wheel
map

5 Ask and answer. Then write a partner's name on their list in 4.

Are you going to take gloves?

Yes, I am. Are you going to take a rope?

No, I'm not.

6 Compare your list with your partner's.

My partner _____ take gloves. My partner _____ take a rope.
I _____ take a map. I _____ take a wheel.
We _____ take _____ .
We _____ take _____ .

I can   talk about future plans using going to .

13

Story lab

READING

I will read a story about an island adventure.

Shipwrecked!

1 Read and circle T (True) or F (False).

1   The children jump out of the boat because the weather is good.   T / F
2   Alice finds Jack because she hears his whistle.   T / F
3   The children think there is water near the trees.   T / F
4   The lighthouse is on the west of the island.   T / F
5   The children leave an SOS message near the river.   T / F

2 Draw the children's route.

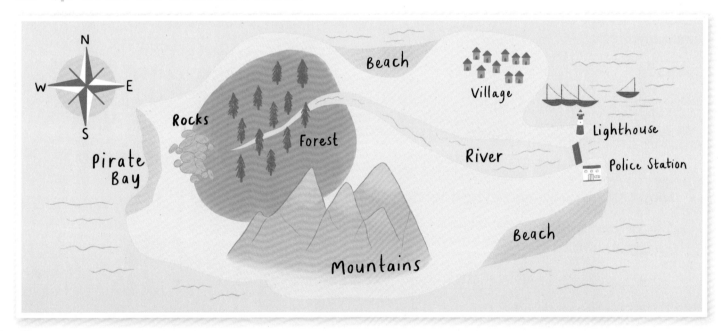

3 Find words in the story that mean …

1   … a type of weather with wind and rain.   _____
2   … a message asking for help.   _____
3   … the way water in a river moves.   _____
4   … when a light goes on and off.   _____
5   … a place that shines a light on the sea at night.   _____
6   … a group of people looking for the children.   _____

4 Read and complete.

> bottle compass knife rocks rope whistle

1 The children make an SOS message with _____ .
2 They climb up the rocks with the _____ .
3 They collect water in a _____ .
4 Alice hears Jack's _____ .
5 Jack cuts open the fruit with a _____ .
6 Alice finds north with a _____ .

5 Read the story review and answer.

Title: Shipwrecked ★ ★ ★ ★ ☆

Main characters: Alice and Jack

Place: an island

Summary: The children are shipwrecked.
They leave a message and find their way across
the island.

Opinion: I think it's an exciting story with
a happy ending.

1 What is the title of the story? _____
2 Who is the story about? _____
3 Where does the story happen? _____
4 What problem have the children got? _____
5 Is the opinion good or bad? _____

6 Write your opinion of the story.

Key	My opinion
1 = very bad	_____
5 = very good	_____

① ② ③ ④ ⑤

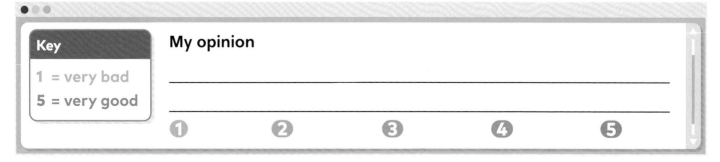

I can read a story about an island adventure.

Experiment lab

ENGINEERING: STRONG BRIDGES

I will learn how to build a bridge.

1 Read and match.

1 Jade Belt Bridge in Beijing is more than 200 years old. It crosses a lake with one high arch. It's only for people.

2 The Braga Bridge crosses the Taunton River in the USA. It's one of the longest truss bridges in the world.

3 The Akashi-Kaiky Bridge in Japan is the longest suspension bridge in the world.

a

b

c

2 Look, read and answer.

MATHS ZONE

BRIDGE
WEIGHT LIMIT
10 TONNES

1600 kg

3000 kg

200 kg

1 There are two lorries on the bridge. How many cars can be on the bridge? _____

2 There are three lorries on the bridge. How many motorbikes can be on the bridge? _____

3 Draw four lines to make the bridge stronger.

How many triangles has the bridge got now? _____

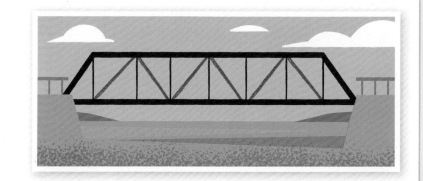

EXPERIMENT TIME

Report

1 Ask and answer. Then complete the table.

How many ice lolly sticks has your bridge got?

It's got ten ice lolly sticks.

Name	Number of ice lolly sticks	Length of bridge	Number of triangles	Number of coins

2 Read and complete.

long   short   stronger   triangles (x3)

1   _____ make a bridge strong.

2   When there are more _____ , the bridge is _____ .

3   A _____ bridge needs more _____ than a _____ bridge.

3 Read and circle. Then discuss with a partner. How difficult was the experiment?

1   Connecting the ice lolly sticks.   Difficult / OK / Easy

2   Using clay.   Difficult / OK / Easy

3   Connecting the triangles.   Difficult / OK / Easy

4   Putting the ruler on the deck.   Difficult / OK / Easy

5   Putting coins on the deck.   Difficult / OK / Easy

Connecting the ice lolly sticks was difficult because they didn't stay in place.

Using clay was easy because I like making things with clay.

I know how to build a bridge.

Time phrases

COMMUNICATION

I will ask and answer about future plans.

1 ☀ Choose and tick ☑ a place and month. Then ask and answer with a partner.

CODE CRACKER ⚙⚙

Holiday options			
Places		**Months**	
Beach camp		June	
Forest camp		July	
River camp		August	

Partner's name:

_____

Place:

_____

Month:

_____

Where are you going on holiday?

When are you going?

I'm going to River camp.

I'm going in July.

2 Complete the email about holiday plans.

To: _____

Subject: Holiday plans

Hi!

I've got my plans ready now!

I'm going to a _____ in _____ .

My friend, _____ , is going to _____ as well!

I'm going to arrive on _____ at _____ .

_____ is going to arrive on _____ at _____ .

I'm going to stay for _____ days. I'm going to leave on

_____ at _____ .

What about you? Where are you going to go on holiday?

From _____

I can ask and answer about future plans.

Writing lab

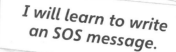

AN SOS MESSAGE

1  Listen to a partner's SOS message and answer.

1   What month is it?   _____

2   Where are they?   _____

3   How long are they going to stay in the same place?   _____

4   Who wrote the message?   _____

2 Look, read and colour.

Key

equipment = ⬤

accident = ⬤

problem = ⬤

place = ⬤

a bike smashed on rocks

a forest with a river

a compass

no food

3 Look at 2. Draw a picture and write an SOS message.

1   Choose a date.

2   Describe the accident and the place.

3   Explain your problem and your plans.

4   Draw a picture of your location.

_____ June

Dear _____ ,

_____

_____

_____

_____

From _____

I **can** write an SOS message.

Plan a class adventure

1 Tick ☑ the things you need for your class adventure.

blanket ☐ boots ☐ bottle ☐ compass ☐ gloves ☐ map ☐

rope ☐ water ☐ wheel ☐ whistle ☐

2 Read and answer about your class adventure.

1 Where are you going to go? _____

2 When are you going to go? _____

3 What are you going to do? _____

3  Listen to the class and choose three class adventures. Then complete the table.

Class adventure	Date	Time of departure	Activities

River Outing!

Date: 27th April

Bus leaves: 9:00 a.m.

Activities: swimming, climbing rocks

Please bring: water, food for lunch, rope, boots, swimming costume

4 Complete the sentences and answer.

difficult   easy   OK

It is _____ working in a group.

It is _____ talking in English.

What did you learn?

1 I learnt _____ .

2 _____

3 _____

I can plan a class adventure.

5 Read and complete.

We're going to the forest on a class adventure.
We're going to leave on Thursday at nine o'clock.
We're going to explore the mountains and make a camp.
I'm going to take a compass, a blanket and a rope.

ADVENTURE PLAN

Place: _____   Day: _____   Time: _____

Activities: _____

Equipment: _____

6 Listen and write the names on the plans.

Sam

Mary

Peter

1 _____

Adventure plan

Place: Beach

Day: Saturday

Time: 8:30

2 _____

Adventure plan

Place: Beach

Day: Friday

Time: 8:00

3 _____

Adventure plan

Place: Forest

Day: Saturday

Time: 9:30

7 Choose a plan from 6 and make a list of equipment. Then ask and answer.

_____ is going to take _____ .

What is Peter going to take on his class adventure?

What is he going to do?

He is going to take a compass.

He is going to explore the beach.

2 Into the past

> How can I make a model of an Aztec city?

1 Read and circle T (True) or F (False).

What do you know about the AZTECS?

1 The Aztecs were from Scotland.   T / F
2 They built big pyramids.   T / F
3 They made plastic jewellery.   T / F
4 There is an Aztec Empire today.   T / F
5 They studied the Sun and the night sky. T / F
6 They used an alphabet for writing.   T / F

2 Read and make the calendar wheels. Then answer the questions.

CODE CRACKER ⚙⚙

THE AZTEC CALENDAR

The Aztecs had two calendars. The most important calendar had 260 days. The Aztecs used it to guess the future.

The calendar had two wheels. The first wheel had numbers from 1 to 13. The second wheel had 20 symbols. The first day in the calendar has got number 1 on the first wheel and the first symbol on the second wheel.

Every day the wheels turn. After 13 days, the first wheel goes back to 1 but now it is with the 14th symbol on the second wheel. After 260 days the two wheels return to their original positions.

On 1st January 2020, the first wheel was on number 10, and the second wheel was on symbol 10.

1 What was the Aztec date on 2nd January 2020?   1st wheel: _____ 2nd wheel: _____
2 What was the Aztec date on 12th January 2020?   1st wheel: _____ 2nd wheel: _____
3 What was the Aztec date on your birthday in 2020?   1st wheel: _____ 2nd wheel: _____

Amazing Aztecs

VOCABULARY

I will learn words to describe life in the past.

1 Unscramble the words, look and complete.

wroe

tae

grwe

deam

ubtli

rkadn

occoa

ryeutk

lsndasa

rellwejye

myipasdr

imzea

1 The Aztecs _____ _____ .

2 They _____ _____ .

3 They _____ _____ .

4 They _____ _____ .

5 They _____ _____ .

6 They _____ _____ .

EXTRA VOCABULARY

2 Look and match.

1 People can get water from wells .

2 A bird has got many feathers .

3 A necklace is a type of jewellery.

4 A tomato is a red fruit.

3 Ph Circle the words that rhyme.

1 here   hair   where   then

2 there   park   pear   ear

3 ate   bear   air   bird

4 chair   cocoa   stand   square

I can use words to describe life in the past.

Language lab

GRAMMAR: PAST AND PRESENT

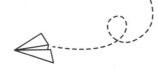

I will learn to compare the past and the present.

1 Read and circle.

AZTEC SPORTS

The Aztecs' favourite sport was / is Ullamaliztli. They play / played in two teams. There are / were four players in each team. The players in the team were / are men. Women don't / didn't play the game. Players didn't / don't use a small ball. They used / use a very heavy ball. The players don't / didn't touch the ball with their hands. They touched / touch the ball with their elbows and knees. They stopped / stop the ball from touching the ground.

In some parts of Mexico today, people play / played a version of the same game. They call / called it 'hip' Ulama because they only touch / touched the ball with their hips. It is / was similar to the original game. They don't / didn't play with women.

2 🔧 008 Listen and complete the notes.

Name of sport: _____

Originally from: _____

Played now: _____

Inside or outside: _____

Because: _____

Number of rules: _____

Equipment: _____

Year of first game: _____

Number of players in first game:

_____

Score in first game: _____

Number of players now: _____

Normal team score: _____

Clothes: _____

3 Use the notes in 2 and the questions. Write a paragraph about basketball.

- Where is basketball from?
- How old is the sport?
- What equipment do you need?
- What is it like now?

Basketball is _____ .

_____

_____

_____

 Gender equality.

 4 💬 **Discuss the questions with a partner.**

Do women do professional sport?

How many women in sport can you name?

Can you name more men than women in sport? Why?

> I can name more men because they are often in the news.

5 💬 **Ask and answer with your partner and complete.**

HOW SPORTY ARE YOU?

❯ Do you do sport every week?	Yes, I do. ☐	No, I don't. ☐
❯ Did you do sport yesterday?	Yes, I did. ☐	No, I didn't. ☐
❯ When did you last do a sport?	_____	
❯ What sport was it?	_____	
❯ Do you watch sport every week?	Yes, I do. ☐	No, I don't. ☐
❯ Did you watch sport last weekend?	Yes, I did. ☐	No, I didn't. ☐
❯ When did you last watch a sport?	_____	
❯ What sport was it?	_____	

> Do you do sport every week?

> Yes, I do.

6 **Compare your partner and yourself.**

I _____ sport every week.   Last week I _____ .

My friend _____ sport every week.   Last week my friend _____ .

 **I can** compare the past and present.

Story lab

I will read a story about a lost treasure.

THE BLACK STONE

1 Read and circle.

1 Why type of objects does Jacobo find in his garden?

   a   plastic rubbish   b   things from the past

2 What type of place does Jacobo live in?

   a   an old town   b   a modern city

3 Where does Jacobo find the black stone?

   a   in his garden   b   near Angie's house

4 What is special about the design on the black stone?

   a   It is very beautiful.   b   The same design is on a building near Angie's house.

5 How do Angie and Jacobo find the door?

   a   They see a black stone under some grass.   b   They see the design on a rock.

6 What is the black stone?

   a   It's a hair decoration.   b   It's a key for the door.

2 Choose and complete. Then number in order.

CODE CRACKER

How do the children find the treasure?   Angie   Jacobo   Jacobo and Angie

a _____ sees a door under some grass. ☐

b _____ find the design on more buildings. ☐

c _____ finds the stone. ☐

d _____ opens the door. ☐

e _____ follow the design on the buildings. ☐

f _____ come to a small hill. ☐

g _____ sees the design on a building. ☐

h _____ clear the grass from the door. ☐

3 Invent and draw your own black stone. Label and describe the design.

My design has got two squares and a circle.

4 Read and tick ☑ the correct summary.

1 This is an adventure story set in modern times. A young boy finds an old stone in his garden. He gives the stone to a friend. ☐

2 This is a fantasy story set in the past. A young boy finds an old stone in his garden. It is the key to a secret door. ☐

3 This is an adventure story set in the past. A young boy finds an old stone in his garden. It is the key to a secret door. ☐

5 Write your opinion of the story.

- Do you like Jacobo and Angie? Why?
- What do you think of the story?

- Do you like the town? Why?

Key	My opinion
1 = very bad 5 = very good	_____

① ② ③ ④ ⑤

I can read a story about a lost treasure.

Experiment lab

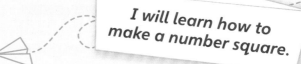

I will learn how to make a number square.

1 **Read and number the texts in order.**

a ☐ But mathematicians in Africa and Spain used different symbols. They used Western Arabic numbers. By the 12th century, mathematicians in many parts of Europe used these symbols.

b ☐ In the sixth century, mathematicians in India invented a symbol for zero. They had a decimal system with 10 numbers. The position of each number showed its value.

c ☐ In the 11th century, many mathematicians in Asia agreed to use the same symbols. They used Eastern Arabic numbers. People in some parts of the world still use these symbols.

d ☐ The history of Arabic numbers

e ☐ In the ninth century, a mathematician wrote a book in Arabic explaining the Indian number system. At that time, there were several different symbols for the numbers.

2 **Listen and number the questions. Then listen again and write the numbers.**

☐ How old are you?

_____ years old

☐ How tall are you?

_____ cm

☐ What's your telephone number?

_____

☐ What bus do you take to school?

_____ bus

☐ How many children go to your school?

_____ children

☐ When were you born?

_____

EXPERIMENT TIME

Report

1 Complete for your number square. Then ask and complete for a partner.

	Me	My partner
What was the number sequence?		
What was the number in the middle?		
What was the sum of the numbers in each row?		

2 Read and circle. Then discuss with a partner. How difficult was the experiment?

1 Understanding the instructions.   Difficult / OK / Easy

2 Drawing the number square.   Difficult / OK / Easy

3 Thinking of the spaces outside the number square.   Difficult / OK / Easy

4 Moving diagonally up and then across.   Difficult / OK / Easy

5 Adding the three numbers in a row.   Difficult / OK / Easy

It's easy to draw the number square because I've got a ruler.

It's difficult to think of spaces outside the number square.

3 Complete the number square and work out the diagonal sum.

MATHS ZONE

		1		15
	5			
		13		22
10				3
		2		

The diagonal sum = _____

I know how to make a number square.

Could and ago

COMMUNICATION

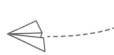

I will ask and answer using **could** and **ago**.

1 Read and write the ages. Then complete the sentences.

Mary, David, Luke and Anna are eight years old.

They could all read and write two years ago.

Mary could first read four years ago.

David couldn't read three years ago.

Two of the children could first read three years ago.

Luke couldn't write three years ago.

David couldn't write before he could read.

Two children could first write three years ago.

Mary

David

Luke

Anna

	Mary	David	Luke	Anna
read				
write				

1 _____ and _____ could first read three years ago.

2 _____ and _____ could first write three years ago.

2 Read and answer. Then find friends with the same answers.

1 I could first read when I was ____ .
That was ____ years ago.

2 I could first write when I was ____ .
That was ____ years ago.

3 I could first walk when I was ____ .
That was ____ years ago.

Could you swim four years ago?

Yes, I could.

No, I couldn't.

3 Write a report for the class.

Read: _____ , _____ and I could read _____ years ago.

Write: _____ , _____ and I could _____ .

Walk: _____

 I can ask and answer using could and ago .

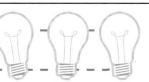

Writing lab

NEWS ARTICLES

I will learn to write a newspaper article.

1 Add punctuation to the sentences.

‘ ’ , .

1 I found the black stone in my garden Jacobo said _____
2 The black stone has got a beautiful design Angie said _____
3 The treasure is more than 500 years old the museum director said _____
4 I think the treasure is very important the museum director said _____
5 Jacobo needs a reward his mother said _____
6 The treasure belongs to the town Jacobo's father said _____

2 Look at the sentences in 1. Write *Fact* or *Opinion*.

3 Choose a treasure and write a newspaper article.

GOLD JEWELLERY IN LOCAL PARK

Ancient compass in forest cave

500-YEAR-OLD BOOK AT SCHOOL JUMBLE SALE

- What does the treasure look like?
- Who found it?
- Where did they find it?
- What is going to happen to the treasure?
- Include quotations with facts and opinions.

HEADLINE

by-line

date

photo

caption

I can write a newspaper article.

PROJECT AND REVIEW UNIT 2

Make a model of an Aztec city

1 Complete the information about your model.

Name of city: _____

Number of pyramids: ____

Number of palaces: ____

Number of small houses: ____

Other places: _____

2 Answer the questions about your building.

1 What type of building did you make? _____

2 What materials did you use? _____

3 Where is your building in the city? _____

3 Ask a partner and take notes.

Where did the family live? _____

What did the father do? _____

What did the mother do? _____

How old were the children? _____

What jewellery did they wear? _____

What did they eat? _____

What did they drink? _____

4 Complete the sentences and answer.   difficult   easy   OK

It is _____ working in a group.   It is _____ talking in English.

What did you learn?

1 I learnt _____ .

2 _____

3 _____

I can make a model of an Aztec city.

5 🎧 010 Listen and write the name.

Atzi   Izel   Patli   Zuma

1 _____   2 _____   3 _____   4 _____

6 Read and create new sentences.

1   Atzi's father worked in a bank.

Atzi's father _____ *didn't work in a bank* _____ . He _____ .

2   Patli's mother didn't have any jewellery.

Zuma's mother _____ . She _____ .

3   Izel's father didn't live in a big house.

_____ . He _____ .

4   Zuma's mother drank cocoa every day.

_____ . She _____ .

7 Choose a character and compare them to yourself.

_____ lived in a _____ . I live in a _____ .

_____ ate _____ . I eat _____ .

_____ drank _____ . I _____ .

8 💬 Ask and guess your partner's character.

Did your character grow maize?

Yes, she did.

1 Checkpoint

1 **Listen and draw a line for Samir. Listen again for Melek. Then answer the questions.**

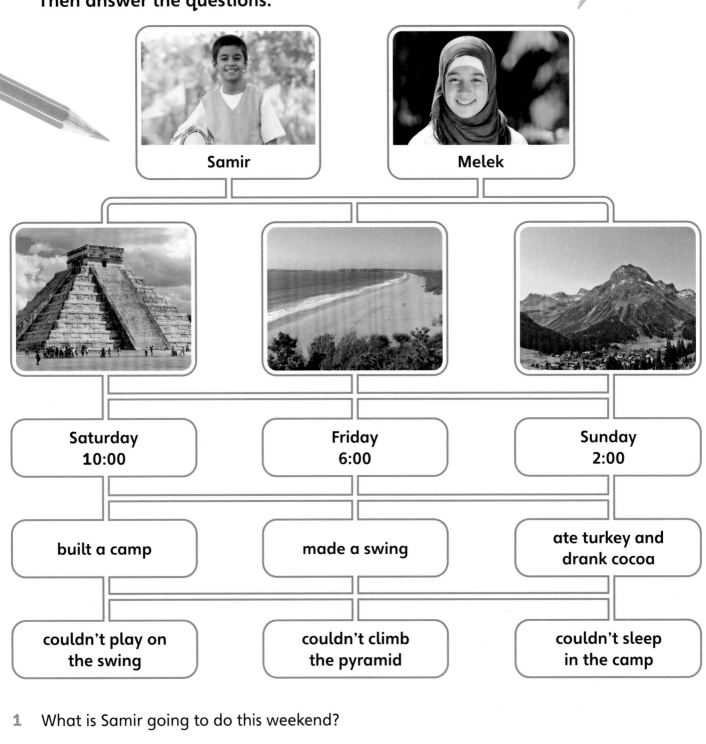

Samir

Melek

Saturday
10:00

Friday
6:00

Sunday
2:00

built a camp

made a swing

ate turkey and
drank cocoa

couldn't play on
the swing

couldn't climb
the pyramid

couldn't sleep
in the camp

1   What is Samir going to do this weekend?

_____

2   What is Melek going to do this weekend?

_____

2 Read and write *true*, *false* or *don't know*.

1 Samir couldn't climb the pyramid five years ago. _____

2 Samir is going to eat turkey and drink cocoa this weekend. _____

3 Samir is going to spend Friday afternoon at the pyramid. _____

4 Melek lives in the mountains. _____

5 Melek is going to have Saturday lunch with her grandparents. _____

6 Melek couldn't sleep in the camp on her last visit. _____

3 Write a paragraph about the last time you visited your favourite place.

Where is your favourite place to visit?   When did you last go?

What did you do?   When are you going to go next?   What are you going to do?

_____

_____

_____

_____

_____

_____

_____

_____

4 Ask a partner about their last visit to their favourite place.

Where's your favourite place?

I like going to the beach.

When did you last go?

I went last summer.

The Saami people

1 Read and answer.

1   What continent is Finland in? _____

2   Why has Finland got days without a night sky? _____

3   What animals do the Saami follow? _____

4   Why do reindeer go north in the summer? _____

5   Where do the Saami live in the summer? _____

2 Read and label.

Description of the Northern Lights
How to see the Northern Lights
Traditional stories   Weather

1 _____ In Finland, you can see lights in the sky on some nights. The colours of the lights are green, yellow, white or red. They move quickly and make amazing shapes in the sky. These are the famous Northern Lights.

2 _____ The Saami people have got many traditional stories about the Northern Lights. In some stories the Northern Lights could talk. In one story, a fire-fox with a long red tail made the red lights. The fire-fox could burn people's hair and so the Saami people wore hats.

3 _____ Some Saami people use the Northern Lights for the weather. Red lights mean it is going to get warmer. White lights mean it is going to get colder. Very high lights mean it is going to snow.

4 _____ The best time to see the Northern Lights is in the winter. Choose a night with no clouds. Go to a place outside the city, with no lights. Look up at the sky and wait!

3 Make a painting of the Northern Lights.

- Cover a piece of paper with red, green and yellow paint.
- Let the paper dry.
- Cover the paint with black crayon.
- Use a spoon and scratch off the black crayon.
- Make a picture to show the Northern Lights.

4 Write a letter to Hugo and tell him about your life. Ask questions about his life, too.

Dear Hugo,

_____

_____

_____

_____

_____

_____

From _____

5 Draw and colour your country's flag. Then describe the flag.

My country's flag is _____

_____ .

It's got _____

_____ .

3 Up into space

How can I design a vehicle for the future?

1 Read and complete.

astronauts   computer   control panel   gravity   handles

_____ train for many months before they go to space.
They practise moving in a zero _____ chamber. They
wear a heavy spacesuit for several hours every day. They use
_____ when they practise space walks. They learn to
use the _____ and to programme the _____ .

2 Listen and tick ☑.

012

IN A SPACECRAFT, THE ASTRONAUTS ...

… play football.	☐	… do experiments. ☐
… eat three meals a day.	☐	… go on spacewalks. ☐
… cook.	☐	… do the cleaning. ☐
… have a shower.	☐	… sleep. ☐

3 Read and number the instructions for a spacewalk.

CODE CRACKER

☐ Use the handles outside the shuttle.
☐ Attach the safety rope.
☐ Check the control panel.
☐ Open the portal.
☐ Put on a spacesuit.
☐ Use the handles inside the shuttle.

Lift off!

VOCABULARY

I will learn words to describe a control panel.

1 Read and complete.

control panel   Earth   engine   fuel
gravity   handles   lights   oxygen
planet   radio   screen   seat

The spacecraft is travelling to another _____ .
The spacecraft has got many parts. It's got an
_____ for firing the shuttle into space. There are _____ tanks for the engine.
There are _____ tanks for breathing. There are a lot of _____ to see the
controls. There's a _____ for the computer and a _____ for communicating with
_____ . There's a _____ for checking supplies. There's a _____ in front of
the instruments for the astronaut. There are _____ for moving in zero _____ .

2 🎧 013 Listen and colour.

```
100%

 80%

 60%

 40%

 20%

       OXYGEN   FUEL   GRAVITY   RADIO   LIGHTS
```

EXTRA VOCABULARY

3 💡 Look and write.

cable   camera   keyboard   screen   USB ports

1 _____
2 _____
3 _____
4 _____
5 _____

4 Ph Complete the riddles. Then tick ☑ the answers.

clear   ear   hear   here
near   year (x2)

1 You can _____ loud and
_____ but it isn't your
_____ . What is it?

 a   a radio ☐
 b   a screen ☐

2 The new _____ is
_____ . The old
_____ is _____ .
What's the date?

 a   31st December ☐
 b   1st January ☐

I can use words to describe a control panel.

Language lab

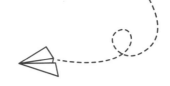

I will learn to talk about the future using **will**.

1  Listen and circle.

A city for the future

1   All buildings in the city will / won't be six floors high.

2   People will / won't grow food on the top of the buildings.

3   People will / won't use water tanks to collect rainwater.

4   The air will / won't be very clean. People will / won't use oxygen tanks.

5   People will / won't use cars. They will / won't travel by bus.

6   People will / won't use plastics. They will / won't recycle food waste.

2 Tick ☑ eight features for a flat in the future.

	bedroom	kitchen	living room	garden
computer				
screen				
radio				
robot				
smart lights				

3 Look at **2** and complete.

CODE CRACKER

My flat

1   The _____ _____ have _____ .

2   The _____ _____ have _____ .

3   The _____ _____ have _____ .

4   The _____ _____ have _____ .

5   The _____ _____ have _____ .

6   The _____ _____ have _____ .

Key

1   ● Use the green words in **2**.

2   ● Use *will* or *won't*.

3   ● Use the blue words in **2**.

4 🗨 Ask and answer with a partner. Take notes.

Name: _____   Features of flat

	bedroom	kitchen	living room	garden
computer				
screen				
radio				
robot				
smart lights				

Will your flat have a robot?

Will the robot be in the garden?

Yes, it will.

No, it won't. It will be in the kitchen.

5 ⚙ Choose a room from your flat. Make a model and write a description.

1 Find a shoebox. Cut off the lid.
2 Cut out the door and the windows.
3 Paint the inside of the box.
4 Use recycled materials to make the furniture, for example, bottle tops, old card, aluminium foil.
5 Paint the furniture. Glue it into position.
6 Use Plasticine for extra features.

My _____

This will be the best _____ in the city.

It will _____ .

It won't _____ .

I made the model with _____ .

I can talk about the future using will .

Story lab

READING

COLONY 369

I will read a story about a space colony.

1 Read and answer.

1   Why are people living in a space colony? _____

2   What is the problem in the space colony? _____

3   Why are the Earth robots worried about the humans? _____

4   Why do the Earth robots open the secret door for the children? _____

5   Where can the children play on Earth? _____

6   What do the adults from Colony 369 promise? _____

2 Read and complete with the number of days.

MATHS ZONE

1   When there are 200 people in the space colony, they've got oxygen for _____ days.

2   When there are 100 people, they've got oxygen for _____ days.

3   When there are 400 people, they've got oxygen for _____ days.

4   When there are 50 people, they've got oxygen for _____ days.

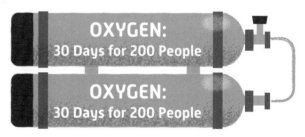

OXYGEN:
30 Days for 200 People

OXYGEN:
30 Days for 200 People

3 Find words in the story that mean ...

1   ... to make very, very dirty.   _____

2   ... a new city a long way from the capital.   _____

3   ... a moving machine with a computer programme.
     It does human tasks.   _____

4   ... to make something so bad it cannot survive.   _____

5   ... to send and receive a message.   _____

6   ... to find a solution.   _____

4 ⚙ Make a promise tree for the future.

1 Use colouring pens to draw a big tree trunk with a lot of branches.

2 Use green paper and cut out leaves.

3 Write a promise for the future on a leaf.

4 Ask your friends and family to write promises on the leaves, too.

5 Glue the leaves on the tree.

5 Complete and circle the story review.

Title: _____

Main characters: _____

Places: _____

Time: future / present / past

Problem:

_____

Solution:

_____

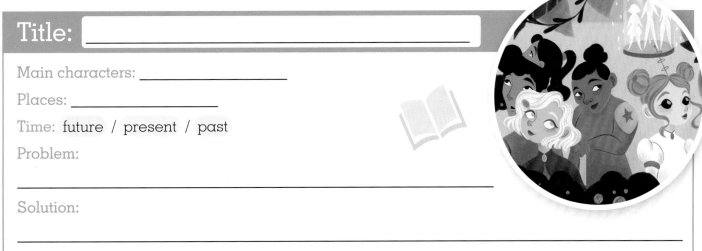

6 Write your opinion of the story.

- Do you like the children in the story? Why / Why not? • What do you think of the story?

- Do you think this will happen in the future? Why / Why not?

Key	My opinion
1 = very bad	_____
5 = very good	_____
	_____
	① ② ③ ④ ⑤

I can read a story about a space colony.

Experiment lab

SCIENCE: SOUND AND COMMUNICATION

I will learn how to make a telephone.

1 Read and match.

WE CAN SHOW SOUND WAVES IN GRAPHS

1 Sound can have a high frequency or pitch. We hear this as a high sound, like a bird. There are a lot of waves in the graph for a high sound. ☐

2 Sound can have a low frequency or pitch. We hear this as a low sound, like the bark of a big dog. There aren't a lot of waves in the graph for a low sound. ☐

3 Sound can be very loud with a high volume. When a sound is loud, the lines on the graph are taller. ☐

4 Sound can be very quiet with a low volume. When a sound is low, the lines on the graph are shorter. ☐

a

b

c

d

2 015 Listen and circle.

1	Pitch:	high / low	Volume:	loud / quiet
2	Pitch:	high / low	Volume:	loud / quiet
3	Pitch:	high / low	Volume:	loud / quiet
4	Pitch:	high / low	Volume:	loud / quiet

3 Draw graphs for the sounds in 2.

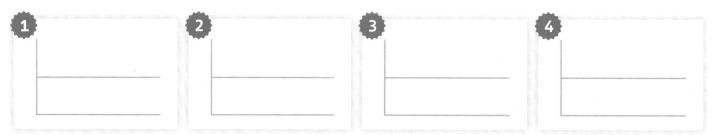

1

2

3

4

4 Read and tick ☑.

When you speak to a deaf person, …

a … look at the person. ☐

b … speak clearly. ☐

c … shout. ☐

5 Sign your name to a partner.

EXPERIMENT TIME

Report

1 Tick ☑ the correct picture and complete the sentences.

❶ ☐

❷ ☐

❸ ☐

Experiment results

My friend can hear me when …

1 _____ .   2 _____ .

> Tying a knot was difficult because I'm not good with my fingers.

2 💬 Read and circle. Then discuss with a partner. How difficult was the experiment?

1 Making a hole in the cup.   Difficult / OK / Easy

2 Tying a knot.   Difficult / OK / Easy

3 Connecting the paper clip.   Difficult / OK / Easy

4 Hearing my partner.   Difficult / OK / Easy

5 Talking into the cup.   Difficult / OK / Easy

I know how to make a telephone.

Questions with *will*

COMMUNICATION

> I will ask and answer about the future using **will**.

1 💡 **Read and tick** ☑ **or cross** ☒ **.**

There are three Eco groups. They all make promises for the future. All the promises are different. All groups will recycle two things. They will only travel one way. They won't use one thing.

▷ **Group A** won't recycle glass. Group C will recycle food and glass. **Group B** won't recycle food.

▷ **Group B** won't travel by foot or by bus. **Group A** will travel with Group B. Group C won't use a vehicle.

▷ Group C will use plastic. **Group A** will use plastic bags, but they won't use plastic bottles. **Group B** will use plastic bottles, but they won't use plastic bags.

	Recycle			Travel by			Use		
	food	glass	paper	foot	bike	bus	plastic bags	cars	plastic bottles
Group A									
Group B									
Group C									

2 ⚙ **Complete your plan. Then ask a partner and take notes.**

FUTURE PLANS

	Me	My partner
Recycle		
Travel by		
Stop using		

> What will you recycle in the future?

> I'll recycle plastic and paper.

I can ask and answer about the future using **will** .

Writing lab

A BROCHURE

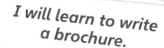
I will learn to write a brochure.

1 **What will it be like in the future? Choose one and discuss.**

a street

a school

a park

a shopping centre

What equipment will there be at a school in the future?

I think there'll be computers for all the students.

2 **Make a brochure and draw a picture for the place you chose in 1.**

_____ FOR THE FUTURE

Name: _____

Location: _____

Inside features: _____

_____

Outside features: _____

_____

3 **Write about the place you chose in 2.**

_____ , there will be _____ .

_____

_____

_____

PROJECT AND REVIEW UNIT 3

Design a vehicle for the future

1 Tick ☑ the features on your vehicle.

computer ☐   engine ☐   handles ☐
lights ☐   radio ☐   screen ☐   seats ☐

(labels on drawings: radio, windows, engine, doors, computer, control panel, seats, wings for flying)

2 Read and answer.

1 How long will the vehicle be?

_____

2 How much will the vehicle weigh?

_____

3 How fast will it go? _____

4 What will be on the control panel? _____

3 Write a description of your vehicle.

Name: _____   It can _____ .

My vehicle is _____ .   _____

On the outside, _____ .   _____

On the inside, _____ .   _____

4 Complete the sentences and answer.

difficult   It is _____ drawing a blueprint.
easy   It is _____ following instructions.
OK   It is _____ talking in English.

What did you learn?

1 I learnt _____ .

2 _____

3 _____

I can design a vehicle for the future.

5 🎧 016 Listen and write the names.

Mark

Anna

Simon

Tessa

_____'S FUTURE PLANS
- live in a space colony
- play inside
- work in the control room

_____'S FUTURE PLANS
- live in a space colony
- work in the vegetable garden
- play inside

_____'S FUTURE PLANS
- live in an underwater city
- work in the vegetable garden
- play outside

_____'S FUTURE PLANS
- live in an underwater city
- work in the control room
- play inside

6 Look at 5. Read and circle T (True) or F (False). Then correct the false sentences.

1 Mark will wear a spacesuit.   T / F _____
2 Anna won't work in the control room.   T / F _____
3 Tessa will play outside.   T / F _____
4 Simon won't wear a swimming costume.   T / F _____
5 Mark won't grow vegetables.   T / F _____
6 Anna will wear a spacesuit.   T / F _____
7 Tessa won't work in a control room.   T / F _____
8 Simon will live underwater.   T / F _____

7 Complete the plans for your future.

IN THE FUTURE
Live: _____
Work: _____
Play: _____

Will you live in this city?

What work will you do?

8 💬 Ask and answer with a partner.

4 Dragons

How can I invent a story about a fantasy animal?

1 Read and answer.

1 What are the children celebrating?

_____

2 What is making the dragon move?

_____

2 Listen and take notes.

1 Dragon flew over: _____

2 Dragon was: _____

3 Dragon wasn't: _____

4 Dragon had: _____

Eva

3 Look, read and complete.

CODE CRACKER

| Key | 1 place | 2 quality | 3 number | 4 colour | 5 body part |

My favourite dragon flew over 1 _____ . It was 2 _____ and

2 _____ . It wasn't 2 _____ .

It had 3 _____ 4 _____ 5 _____ and 3 _____ 4 _____

5 _____ .

4 Make a dragon mask.

1 Paint a paper plate the colour of your dragon.

2 Draw and cut out two circles for the eyes.

3 Paint a nose and mouth.

4 Cut strips of coloured paper and glue them to your mask.

5 Make a hole on each side of the plate and put a piece of elastic through.

Dragons around the world

VOCABULARY

I will learn words to describe dragons.

1 Choose and write. Then write the words in the past.

1   to move in water   _____ _____

2   to move in the air   _____ _____

3   to make fire and smoke   _____ _____

4   something we do in bed every night   _____ _____

5   to move slowly on land   _____ _____

burn
fly
sleep
swim
walk

2 018 Listen and number. Then choose and describe.

☐ strong, dangerous, from the west

☐ strong, brave, from the north

☐ dangerous, brave, from the east

This dragon was _____ .   It wasn't _____ .

It slept _____ .   It didn't _____ .

EXTRA VOCABULARY

3 Write the words in bold next to the meanings.

This dragon **guarded** a big treasure. He was very **greedy**.

This dragon **taught** people to read. He was very **wise**.

1   teachers did this in the past   _____

2   wanting a lot of food, jewellery and gold   _____

3   knowing a lot about the world   _____

4   didn't stop watching the treasure   _____

 I can   use words to describe dragons.

Language lab

GRAMMAR: ACTIVITIES IN THE PAST

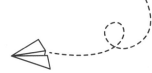

I will learn to talk about activities in the past.

1 **Listen and complete the times.**

	yellow dragon	red dragon
started burning the forest	__ : __	__ : __
stopped burning the forest	__ : __	__ : __
started swimming in the lake	__ : __	__ : __
stopped swimming in the lake	__ : __	__ : __

2 **Look at 1. Read and complete.**

> burning the forest   swimming in the lake   was (x4)   wasn't (x4)   were   weren't

1 At 7:00, the yellow dragon _____ . It wasn't _____ .
2 At 9:00, the red dragon _____ . It _____ .
3 At 5:00, the yellow dragon _____ . It _____ .
4 At 4:00, the red dragon _____ . It _____ .
5 At 8:00, both dragons _____ . They _____ .

3 **Look at 1. Colour the clocks and write the minutes.**

MATHS ZONE

1 How long was the yellow dragon burning the forest for? _____ minutes

2 How long was the red dragon burning the forest for? _____ minutes

3 How long were both dragons burning the forest for? _____ minutes

4 How long was the yellow dragon swimming in the lake for? _____ minutes

52

4 Choose a dragon and complete the times.

2:00–3:30   10:00–11:30   12:00–1:30

	My dragon: _____		My partner's dragon: _____	
	Start time	Stop time	Start time	Stop time
eating	[__ __ : __ __]	[__ __ : __ __]	[__ __ : __ __]	[__ __ : __ __]
flying	[__ __ : __ __]	[__ __ : __ __]	[__ __ : __ __]	[__ __ : __ __]
sleeping	[__ __ : __ __]	[__ __ : __ __]	[__ __ : __ __]	[__ __ : __ __]

5 Use the times to ask and answer with a partner. Complete their times in 4.

1:00   3:00   11:00

Was your dragon eating at three o'clock?

Was it eating at 11 o'clock?

No, it wasn't.

Yes, it was.

6 Imagine you were with the dragons. Read and answer.

1   Where was your dragon when it was eating?

_____

2   What was it eating?

_____

3   What were you doing when it was eating?

_____

4   When was your dragon flying over the village?

_____

5   Where was it going?

_____

6   What were you doing when it was flying over the village?

_____

 talk about activities in the past.

Story lab

READING

I will read a story about good and bad dragons.

A TALE OF TWO DRAGONS

1 Read and answer.

1 What were the people doing at the start of the story?

_____

2 What was the weather like?

_____

3 Where did the fire dragon come from?

_____

4 Why were the people scared of the dragon?

_____

5 Why did the water dragon wake up?

_____

6 Which dragon was stronger? Why?

_____

2 Find words in the story that ...

1   ... start a traditional story.   _____

2   ... show the fire dragon is dangerous.   _____

3   ... show the water dragon controls the weather.   _____

4   ... show the mountain is a volcano.   _____

3 Find the words in the story and complete the sentences.

1 _____ came from the dragon's mouth and burnt all the trees in the forest.

2 They were _____ with very loud voices.

3 The children made a very loud _____ .

4 The dragon stopped sleeping and _____ .

5 A small collection of houses is a _____ .

6 Water can _____ a fire.

4 Cross ☒ the events that do not answer the question. Then number the events in order.

HOW DID THE FIRE DRAGON GET INTO THE MOUNTAIN CAVE?

A ☐ The water dragon used a rock for the cave's door.

B ☐ The people ran to the beach.

C ☐ The water dragon made rain.

D ☐ The water dragon put the fire dragon in a cave.

E ☐ All the people in the village shouted.

F ☐ The fire dragon burnt the forest.

G ☐ The water dragon chased the fire dragon.

H ☐ The water dragon woke up.

I ☐ A girl shouted.

5 Complete the story review.

1 What are the people doing at the start of the story?

_____

2 What problem have they got? _____

3 What solution do they find? _____

Title: _____

Type of story: _____

Fantasy characters: _____

Place: _____

6 Write your opinion of the story.

- Why is the girl in the story important?
- Is the explanation real?
- What does the story explain?
- What do you think of the story?

● ● ●

Key	My opinion
1 = very bad	_____
5 = very good	_____
	_____
	① ② ③ ④ ⑤

I can read a story about good and bad dragons.

Experiment lab

SCIENCE: FLYING MACHINES

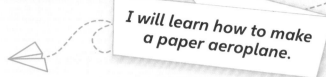

I will learn how to make a paper aeroplane.

1 **Read, choose and write.**

In-flight entertainment   Passengers   Price   Space

COMMERCIAL AIR TRAVEL

1 _____ Commercial aeroplanes are very different than they were 100 years ago. The first commercial aeroplane flew in 1914. It only took one passenger. In the 1920s, aeroplanes took between 10 and 12 passengers. By the end of the century, the largest commercial aeroplanes carried around 400 passengers.

2 _____ In the 1920s, commercial flights were very expensive. By the 1950s, more people were travelling by aeroplane because they were bigger and so prices came down. In the 1980s, there were a lot of cheap airlines.

3 _____ The first commercial flights didn't have screens or radios and people ate big meals. By the 1960s, passengers had screens on long flights and they had free meals, too! By 2010, aeroplanes had internet connection, music and a lot of films.

4 _____ In the 1920s, passengers didn't sit in rows. They had round tables and a lot of space. In the 1960s, passengers still had a lot of room for their legs. With cheap prices in the 1980s, there were more passengers and there wasn't as much space.

2 **Look at 1. Read, choose and write.**

1923   1965   1987   2015

1   I was reading emails on the flight.   _____

2   We sang songs because there wasn't a radio or screen.   _____

3   I didn't like the film, but the free meal was very good.   _____

4   The flight was very cheap, but there wasn't much space.   _____

3 **Write about a journey in an aeroplane.**

I went on a flight from _____ to _____ . I was flying from [_:_] to [_:_]. The aeroplane had _____ , _____ and _____ . On the flight, I _____ .

Understand fears.

4 Imagine you were on a long flight last weekend. Do the quiz.

Are you AFRAID OF FLYING?

1 Did you sleep on the flight?   a No   b A bit   c A lot
2 Did you listen to the safety advice?   a Yes   b No
3 Were you breathing quickly at any moment?   a Yes   b No
4 Were you scared of the aeroplane's movements?   a No   b A bit   c A lot
5 Do you understand how an aeroplane stays in the air?   a No   b A bit   c A lot
6 Are you scared of small spaces?   a No   b A bit   c A lot

Points: 1 a 5, b 3, c 0; 2 a 0, b 5; 3 a 5, b 0; 4 a 0, b 3, c 5; 5 a 5, b 3, c 0; 6 a 0, b 3, c 5

ANSWER KEY: **0–10:** You are not scared of flying.   **11–20:** You are sometimes scared.   **21–30:** You don't like flying very much. Learn more about aeroplanes!

EXPERIMENT TIME

Report

1 Complete the sentences.

Aeroplane average time in air: 🕐 1 _____ + 🕐 2 _____ + 🕐 3 _____ = _____ / 3 = _____

Aeroplane average distance: 📏 1 _____ + 📏 2 _____ + 📏 3 _____ = _____ / 3 = _____

In my group, the _____ aeroplane travelled the longest distance.

In my group, the _____ aeroplane travelled in the air for the longest time.

2 Read and circle. Then discuss with a partner. How difficult was the experiment?

1 Following the instructions.   Difficult / OK / Easy
2 Folding the paper.   Difficult / OK / Easy
3 Throwing the aeroplane.   Difficult / OK / Easy
4 Measuring the distance.   Difficult / OK / Easy
5 Timing the flight.   Difficult / OK / Easy

> Following the instructions was easy because of the pictures.

I know how to make a paper aeroplane.

Events in the past

COMMUNICATION

I will ask and answer about events in the past.

1 🔄 Listen and match.

At the party ...

1 Jack

2 Bill and Mary

3 Saskia

4 Mary and Saskia

5 Jack

6 Bill

was

were

swimming in the lake

playing a game

eating an apple

when

the aeroplane landed.

the music started.

the police arrived.

2 Imagine you were at the party. Read and answer.

1 What were you doing when the aeroplane landed?

_____

2 What were you doing when the music started?

_____

3 What were you doing when the police arrived?

_____

3 💬 Ask and answer with a partner. Take notes.

Name: _____
What were you doing when the ...
... aeroplane landed?   _____
... music started?   _____
... police arrived?   _____

What were you doing when the police arrived?

I was walking in the garden.

 I can ask and answer about events in the past.

Writing lab

A WITNESS STATEMENT

> I will learn to write a witness statement.

PRACTISE YOUR WITNESS SKILLS!

- Are you a good witness? A good witness notices a lot of details.
- What can you remember about the start of the school day?
- Good questions can help a witness to remember details.

1 Read and answer.

1 What time did you arrive in your classroom? _____

2 How many people were in the classroom? _____

3 What were they doing? _____

4 When did your teacher arrive? _____

5 What were you doing? _____

2 Choose an event and write questions to ask a partner.

The lights went out. ☐   The fire alarm started. ☐   The computer burnt. ☐

1 What were _____ ?   2 What did _____ ?

3 Who were _____ ?   4 Where were _____ ?

5 When did _____ ?

3 ✺ Ask a partner the questions from 2.

What were you doing when the fire alarm started?

I was reading a book.

4 Complete a witness statement for your partner.

Name: _____

Date: _____

Event: _____

_____ was _____

when _____ .

He / She was with _____ .

Then he / she _____ .

I can write a witness statement.

PROJECT AND REVIEW UNIT 4

Invent and tell a story about a fantasy animal

Project report

1 Make a sock puppet of your fantasy animal.

1 Find a long sock of the same colour as your fantasy animal.
2 Glue buttons on for the eyes.
3 Add special features with ribbons, coloured paper and wool.
4 Put your hand in the sock and make your fantasy animal talk.

2 Complete the description.

My fantasy animal is called _____ . It was from _____ . It had
_____ . It could _____ . It couldn't _____ . I made
the sock puppet with _____ .

3 Answer the questions about the story.

1 What was your fantasy animal doing at the start? _____
2 Who did your fantasy animal meet? _____
3 What was the friend doing? _____
4 Where were they? _____
5 What did they do next? _____

4 Complete the sentences and answer.

difficult   easy   OK

It is _____ inventing details of a fantasy animal.
It is _____ writing in English.
It is _____ reading the story out loud.

What did you learn?
1 I learnt _____ .
2 _____
3 _____

I can invent and tell a story about a fantasy animal.

5 Listen and write the names.

	a dragon flew overhead	the fire started	the village burnt
swimming in the lake			
walking in the forest			
sleeping			
reading a book			

Luis

Melek

Yanyu

Carol

6 Read and tick ☑ the true sentences. Correct the false sentences.

1   Luis wasn't walking in the forest when the dragon flew overhead.   ☐

2   Melek and Carol were swimming in the lake when the fire started.   ☐

3   Yanyu was reading a book when the village burnt.   ☐

4   Melek wasn't reading a book when a dragon flew overhead.   ☐

5   Luis and Carol weren't walking in the forest when the fire started.   ☐

6   Luis was sleeping when a dragon flew overhead.   ☐

_____

_____

_____

_____

7 Choose an activity for each event in 5 and write your name. Then describe your day.

I was _____ when _____ . I wasn't _____ .

I was _____ when _____ . I wasn't _____ .

I was _____ when _____ . I wasn't _____ .

8 Look at 5 and 7. Ask and answer with a partner.

What were you doing when a dragon flew overhead?

I was swimming in the lake.

Now go to your Progress Chart on page 4.

2 Checkpoint

UNITS 3 AND 4

1 🎧 022 **Listen and draw lines for Ana. Listen again for Luis. Then complete the sentences.**

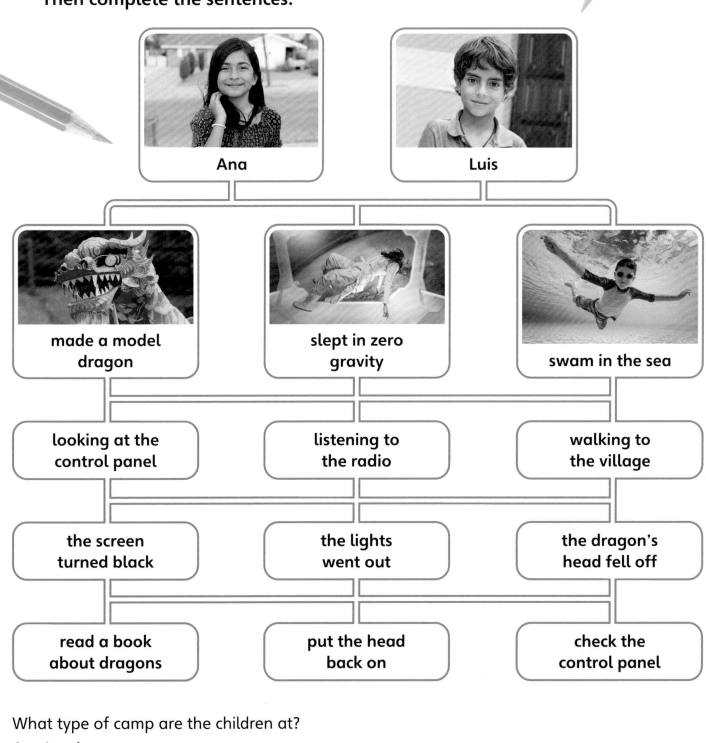

Ana

Luis

made a model dragon

slept in zero gravity

swam in the sea

looking at the control panel

listening to the radio

walking to the village

the screen turned black

the lights went out

the dragon's head fell off

read a book about dragons

put the head back on

check the control panel

What type of camp are the children at?

1   Ana is at a _____ camp.

2   Luis is at a _____ camp.

2 Read and write *true*, *false* or *don't know*.

1 Ana didn't sleep in a bed yesterday. _____

2 Luis was walking to the village when the dragon's head fell off. _____

3 Ana was looking at a screen when it turned red. _____

4 The control panel needs fixing. _____

5 The model dragon can fly. _____

6 Luis will watch a film about dragons. _____

3 Imagine what your life will be like in the future. Write a paragraph.

Ana wants to be an astronaut. In the future, she'll fly a rocket and she'll explore the planets.

What about you?   What will you be?   Where will you live?

Who will you live with?   What will your city be like?

4 Ask a partner what their life will be like in the future.

Will you be an astronaut in the future?

No, I won't.

Where will you live?

I think I'll live in a different country.

1 What can we call Panama? Read and tick ☑.

1 Home of the west wind ☐

2 Bridge of the Americas ☐

3 Land of the dragons ☐

Panama is a long, narrow country. It is between the Atlantic and the Pacific oceans. It is one of several countries between North and South America. It's got two oceans.

2 Read and number in order.

☐ The Guna moved out of the jungle because many people were getting ill. _____ When the Europeans arrived in the area in the 17th century, the Guna were farming and fishing along the coast.

☐ Life for the Guna will be different in the future. The weather is getting warmer, there is more water in the seas and the islands are getting smaller. Soon, there won't be a lot of space on the islands for the Guna people. Some people will have to leave the island. _____

☐ **The Guna people: past and future**

The Guna people originally came from the mainland of Panama. _____ They lived in the jungle. Their villages were near rivers and they fished and hunted for their food.

☐ The Guna people adapted in the past and they will adapt in the future. They won't forget their traditions. There will be culture classes. _____ They'll find out about the traditional way of life when they visit their family on the islands for holidays. And their parents will speak the Guna language at home and tell them the traditional stories.

☐ The Guna moved their house to the islands of Panama at the start of the 19th century. They still farmed on the mainland, but they lived on the islands. They wanted to keep their traditions and language. _____

3 Look at 2. Read again and add the missing sentences.

a   The children will learn Guna music and dance.

b   They travelled down the rivers to the coast.

c   They'll go and live in the capital city.

d   They didn't live on the islands.

e   For many years, only the Guna could visit the islands.

4 Complete the sentences with *will* or *won't*.

In the city …

1   the Guna _____ live in flats.

2   they _____ live in huts.

3   they _____ go fishing every day.

4   they _____ travel by bus or car every day.

5   they _____ do many different jobs.

5 Imagine you are a Guna child. Is it better to live in the city or on the islands? Discuss with a partner.

> In the city, the children will live in flats, not in huts.

> Yes, but they won't go fishing every day in the city.

6 Write a summary of a traditional story.

Think of a traditional story from your country about the Moon or stars.

What were the characters doing at the start of the story? How did they change in the story?

Title: _____   Characters: _____   Place: _____

At the start of the story: _____

At the end of the story: _____

7  Make a bookmark.

1   Choose your favourite character from the traditional story.

2   Cut out the face from card.

3   Use buttons and thread for the eyes and hair.

4   Glue the face to the top of the stick.

5   Write the name of the story on the stick.

 about culture in Panama.

5 Endangered animals

How can I organise a campaign to save an animal?

1 🎧 023 Listen and sort.

> bats   dogs   donkeys   elephants
> goats   hamsters   horses   otters
> owls   rabbits   sharks

Endangered
_____
_____
_____

Some are endangered
_____
_____
_____

Not endangered
_____
_____
_____

2 Label the word groups. Then choose and complete.

CODE CRACKER ⚙️⚙️

> endangered animals   habitats   threats

1 _____ : air pollution
  water pollution   chemicals
2 _____ : donkeys   elephants
  otters   sharks
3 _____ : sea   field   forest

_____ live in the _____ .
_____ is a problem for _____ .

3 Complete the wildlife observation sheet.

Wildlife Observation Sheet

Place: _____

Date: _____

Habitat: _____
_____

Animals: _____
_____

Threats: _____
_____

Wonderful wildlife

VOCABULARY

I will learn animal and habitat words.

1 Unscramble the letters and complete the sentences.

lsemicah _____

battiha _____

rutelt _____

nausnmtio _____

hatetr _____

futyelbtr _____

flwo _____

regit _____

alege _____

lotpluoni _____

defil _____

terot _____

1 A _____ is habitat with a lot of grass.

2 A _____ looks like a dog, but is a wild animal.

3 A _____ has got a shell on its back.

4 A _____ is something that puts animals in danger.

5 An _____ is an animal that lives near rivers.

6 A _____ has got colourful wings.

7 _____ on plants are a threat to wildlife.

8 A _____ looks like a cat, but is big and dangerous.

9 A forest is a type of _____ .

10 An _____ is a bird with big wings.

11 _____ makes the air, land or water dirty.

12 _____ are high and rocky habitats.

EXTRA VOCABULARY

2 🎧 024 Match the habitats to the animals. Then listen and check.

Arctic   grasslands   tundra   wetlands

wolves: _____

birds with long legs:

_____

polar bears: _____

elephants: _____

3 Ph Make words.

The second letter in all the words is *r*.

How many words can you make?

_____

_____

_____

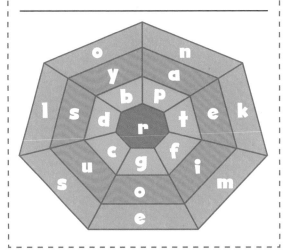

Language lab

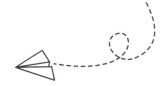
GRAMMAR: *IF* ... SENTENCES

1 025 **Listen and complete with will or won't.**

GREEN CITY 10-year Plan

1   We _____ have a nature reserve.

2   There _____ be a lot of trees.

3   There _____ be fish in the river.

4   There _____ be fields for vegetable gardens.

5   People _____ use chemicals.

6   There _____ be any cars in the city centre.

7   Shops _____ have plastic bags.

8   There _____ be rubbish bins on every street.

2 **Match the ideas to the sentences in 1.**

☐ cleaner streets   ☐ a good diet   ☐ a lot of wildlife

☐ less plastic waste   ☐ no pollution in the air ☐ cleaner air

☐ more otters   ☐ a lot of butterflies

3 **Complete the sentences. Write two endings using will and won't.**

1   If there aren't any cars, ____*we will use bikes*____ / __*we won't need petrol stations*__ .

2   If there are a lot of trees, _____ / _____ .

3   If there are a lot of rubbish bins, _____ / _____ .

4   If there are vegetable gardens, _____ / _____ .

4 Read and draw a path.

Example answer

Read the condition.

Choose a positive ➕ and a negative ➖ from Result 1 and connect with lines.

Think of a positive ➕ and a negative ➖ for Result 2, connect with lines and complete.

> **Condition:** If they make a new park, …
>
> **Result 1:** ➕ place for biking   ➕ playground   ➖ no shops   ➖ dangerous at night
>
> **Result 2:** ➕ _more exercise_   ➖ _less choice_

> **Condition:** If they make a new park, …
>
> **Result 1:** ➕ place for biking   ➕ playground   ➖ no shops   ➖ dangerous at night
>
> **Result 2:** ➕ _____   ➖ _____

---

5 Choose one condition and four results. Then complete the path.

CODE CRACKER ⚙️⚙️

> more houses
> new hospital
> new nature reserve

> a lot of insects   chemicals   dangerous animals
> good for families   good for fruit   good for wildlife
> more doctors   more pollution   more roads   pollution in the air

> **Condition:** If _____
>
> **Result 1:** ➕ _____   ➖ _____
>
> **Result 2:** ➕ _____   ➖ _____

---

6 💬 Talk to a partner about your path in 5.

> If they build a new hospital, they will build more roads.

> If they build more roads, there will be more cars.

I can use sentences with _if_.

Story lab

READING

I will read a story about looking after animals.

Aset and Kara

1 Read and answer.

1 How does Aset find Kara?

_____

_____

2 What animal does Aset think he's got? Why?

_____

_____

3 How does Aset look after Kara?

_____

_____

4 How do Aset's mum and dad feel about Kara?

_____

5 How does Aset help Kara to find her mother?

_____

6 Why does Aset's mum get a grey puppy?

_____

2 Read and complete with *dogs* or *wolves*.

1 We can train _____ .

2 _____ eat sheep.

3 _____ can be small or big.

4 _____ are dangerous.

5 _____ live with humans.

6 _____ live with other wolves.

3 Find words in the story that mean ...

1 ... a very young dog. _____

2 ... have something for yourself. _____

3 ... talked in a very quiet voice. _____

4 ... a building for farm produce. _____

5 ... gave food. _____

6 ... ran after something. _____

7 ... dragging something behind you. _____

8 ... communicated over a long distance. _____

4  Make a model of a habitat.

1   Make a mountain by gluing balls of paper together. Stick it to a piece of card.

2   Use small card boxes for houses and glue them on or around the mountain.

3   Make a paste by mixing one cup of water and one cup of flour.

4   Cut paper into strips and dip the paper in the paste.

5   Cover the mountain and small boxes with the strips.

6   When it is dry, paint the mountain and the houses.

5 Complete and circle the story review.

Title: _____   ★ ★ ★ ★ ★

Main characters: _____   Places: _____

Type of story: science fiction / modern day / historical

Main event at the start: _____

Events in the middle: _____

Problem: _____

Solution for Kara: _____

Solution for Aset: _____

6 Write your opinion of the story.

- How can you describe Aset?
- Do you think it is a realistic story? Why?
- Do you like him? Why?
- What do you think of the story?

Key	My opinion
1 = very bad	_____
5 = very good	_____
	_____
	① ② ③ ④ ⑤

I can read a story about looking after animals.

Experiment lab

ART AND DESIGN: LIGHT BOXES

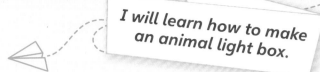

I will learn how to make an animal light box.

1 Read and complete.   bones   glass   paper   wood

Light boxes make pictures using shadows and light. Light passes though the box and the objects inside the box block the light and make shadows. Light can pass through some materials, like _____ and _____ . Other materials block the light, like _____ and _____ .

2 Read and complete with *front* or *back*.

Shadow puppets

Around the world people use light boxes and shadow puppets for telling stories. At the _____ of the light box, there is a screen of thin paper, and at the _____ , there are some lights. The big objects, like mountains or big buildings, are at the _____ of the light box, and the small objects, like trees or houses, are at the _____ . The puppets can move around in the light box, from the _____ to the _____ . A person at the _____ of the light box moves the sticks or strings to make the puppets move.

3 💡 **Colour the mountains yellow in the light and black in the shadow. Then read and complete.**

Morning   Afternoon   Evening

afternoon   bottom (x2)   evening   left   middle   morning   right   top

1   In the _____ scene, the light is at the _____ in the _____ .

2   In the _____ scene, the light is at the _____ in the _____ .

3   In the _____ scene, the light is at the _____ in the _____ .

4 Describe your light box.

- Can you think of a title?
- What is at the front and back of the light box?
- What habitat and animals can you see?

Title: _____

_____

_____

5 🗨 **Ask and answer with a partner.**

> What habitat can you see in your light box?

> It's a forest habitat.

EXPERIMENT TIME

Report

1 Answer the questions about your light box.

1 Is the light stronger at the front or the back? Why?

_____

2 Are the colours darker at the front or the back? Why?

_____

3 What are the positive shapes?

_____

4 What are the negative shapes?

_____

5 What colour are the lights?

_____

2 🗨 Read and circle. Then discuss with a partner. How difficult was the experiment?

1 Following the instructions.	Difficult / OK / Easy
2 Making the box.	Difficult / OK / Easy
3 Cutting out positive shapes.	Difficult / OK / Easy
4 Cutting out negative shapes.	Difficult / OK / Easy
5 Making holes in the cardboard.	Difficult / OK / Easy
6 Putting the 3D picture inside the box.	Difficult / OK / Easy
7 Gluing the LED strip in place.	Difficult / OK / Easy
8 Switching on the light.	Difficult / OK / Easy

> Cutting out positive shapes was easy because you can cut from the outside.

I know how to make an animal light box.

More or fewer?

I will describe quantities using **more** and **fewer**.

1 Look and complete.

bears   fewer   more   otters   wolves

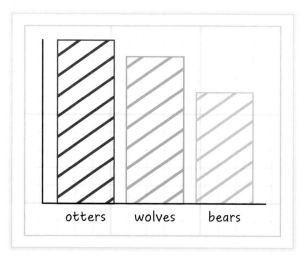

1   There are _____ bears than _____ .
2   There are _____ bears than _____ .
3   There are _____ wolves than _____ .
4   There are _____ wolves than _____ .
5   There are _____ otters than _____ .
6   There are _____ otters than _____ .

otters   wolves   bears

2 Work with a partner. Each choose a habitat and complete. Then ask and answer.

Habitat	Number of types of ...			
	butterflies	otters	eagles	bears
mountain				
river				

How many types of butterflies are there in your habitat?

There are five types of butterflies.

3 Compare the habitats in 2 and complete the report.

Wildlife Report

In the mountain habitat, there are _____ than _____ .
In the river habitat, there are _____ than _____ .
In the mountain habitat, there are _____ than _____ .
In the river habitat, there are _____ than _____ .
In the mountain habitat, there are _____ than _____ .
In the river habitat, there are _____ than _____ .

I can describe quantities using more and fewer .

Writing lab

I will learn to write a letter.

A LETTER

1 Read, choose and write.

Key   P: Problem   R: Results   S: Solution

1 no trees in park for birds to build nests ☐

2 plant more trees in the park ☐

3 fewer birds ☐

Values Communicate with respect.

2 Read and match.

There are different ways to start a letter or an email. The relationship between two people is important.

1 to an unknown person ●   ● Hi there!
2 an informal letter or email ●   ● Dear Juan,
3 a formal letter or email ●   ● Dear Sir or Madam,
4 to a close friend ●   ● Dear Mr Smith,

3 Write a letter.

Choose a problem and a person.
Think of two results and suggest a solution.

plan to build 200 houses near a nature reserve
plan to close down an animal sanctuary
the park keeper   your friend   your headteacher

4 Listen to a partner's letter and take notes.

Problem: _____

Results: _____

Solution: _____

I can write a letter.

Organise a campaign to save an animal

Project report

1 Answer the questions about your campaign.

1 Which animal did you choose?

_____

2 Where is it from?

_____

3 What type of habitat does it live in?

_____

4 Why is it in danger?

_____

2 Complete the information about your campaign.

People in the group: _____

Actions: _____ made _____ . _____ used _____ .

_____ made _____ . _____ used _____ .

_____ wrote _____ .

Presentation: _____ showed _____ .

_____ explained _____ . _____ read _____ .

3 Read and number. Answer and discuss.

Key   1 = very easy   10 = very difficult

Finding a list of endangered animals. ☐

Working in a group. ☐   Finding out why the animals are endangered. ☐

Making a list of campaign actions. ☐   Finding the materials. ☐

Presenting the campaign. ☐   Making one of the campaign actions. ☐

What did you learn?

1 I learnt _____ .

2 _____

3 _____

I can organise a campaign to save an animal.

4 Listen and draw four paths using different colours.

| If they build a new city, … | | If they make a new lake, … |

cut down a lot of trees

more otters

more fish

not a lot of oxygen

no habitat for animals

children have no place to play

people have health problems

no playground

endangered animals

5 Look at 4 and answer the questions.

1   What will happen if they build a new city?

If they build a new city, _____ .

_____

_____

2   What will happen if they make a new lake?

If they make a new lake, _____ .

_____

_____

6 Choose and write about a habitat using **more** and **fewer**.

	mountain	forest	river
eagles	60	30	10
otters	10	20	50
bats	20	70	30

In the _____ habitat, there are _____ bats than otters.

There are _____ .

There are _____ .

7 Ask and guess a partner's habitat.

Are there more otters or bats?

Are there fewer otters or eagles?

That's the river habitat!

There are more otters.

There are fewer eagles.

6 Join in!

How can I have a club fair?

1 🎧 027 Listen and tick ☑ the true sentences.

1   Chunhua is going to the city with her school friends. ☐

2   She's going to stay for two days. ☐

3   She's going to stay for one day. ☐

4   She's going to take part in a chess competition. ☐

5   She's going to do gymnastics. ☐

6   She's going to sing with a choir. ☐

7   She's going to meet her family. ☐

Chunhua is going to celebrate Children's Day.

2 How do you celebrate Children's Day? Circle and complete.

We take part in competitions, do gymnastics, sing with a choir, walk with friends, have an art exhibition. We _____ .

3 💡 Read and sort the number of children in each group.

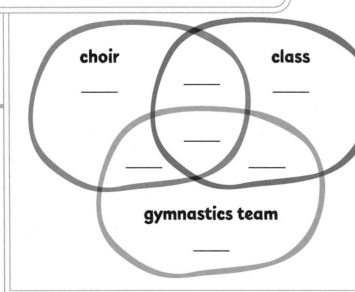

choir
_____

class
_____ _____

_____

_____ _____

gymnastics team
_____

CODE CRACKER

There are 20 children in my class.

Five of my friends are in the choir with me.

There are 15 people in the choir.

I'm in the gymnastics team as well.

There are 10 people in the gymnastics team. Four of us are from my class.

Two people from the gymnastics team are in the choir, but they aren't in our class.

Join a club!

VOCABULARY

I will learn club activity words.

1 Read and match.

1   find and like new people
2   decide on a time to see a friend
3   be in an activity or event
4   an area of a city or town
5   a group of people who sing together
6   a board game for two people
7   if you practise, you will …
8   someone will win this

- get better
- chess
- make new friends
- take part
- contest
- meet a friend
- neighbourhood
- choir

EXTRA VOCABULARY

2 Read, look and label. Use the words in bold.

Archery is a sport you do outside on your own.
Skiing is a winter sport.

In **programming** classes, children design new games.
Ballet is a popular type of dance.

_____ _____ _____ _____

3 Ph Find paths and write the words.

Start with the letter *s*.
You can go backwards or forwards.
You cannot use the same letter twice.
How many words can you make?

_____

_____

Language lab

GRAMMAR: *SHOULD, ALWAYS* OR *NEVER*

1 Label the places and complete the rules with should or shouldn't.

> library   swimming pool

1

_____

You _____ talk.

You _____ run.

You _____ look at the books.

2

_____

You _____ bring a towel.

You _____ run.

You _____ push.

2 Listen and tick ☑. Then answer the question.

		always	often	sometimes	never
1	meet outside				
2	visit museums				
3	use crayons				
4	make 3D objects				
5	bring materials				
6	put away the equipment				

Tarek

What is Tarek's club? _____

3 Look at 2. Read and circle T (True) or F (False).

1   The group always meet inside.   T / F

2   The group sometimes visit museums.   T / F

3   Tarek sometimes uses crayons.   T / F

4   Tarek never makes 2D pictures.   T / F

5   The art club has always got paper and crayons.   T / F

6   Tarek is often lazy.   T / F

Help at home.

4 Read, circle and complete. Then add up your points and compare the results.

WHAT TASKS DO YOU DO AT HOME?

1 Do you make your bed in the morning?	always	often	sometimes	never
2 Do you do the washing-up in the evening?	always	often	sometimes	never
3 Do you put away your toys?	always	often	sometimes	never
4 Do you empty the bins?	always	often	sometimes	never
5 Do you tidy your bedroom?	always	often	sometimes	never
6 Do you clean the bathroom?	always	often	sometimes	never

Points: always = 3, often = 2, sometimes = 1, never = 0   My result: _____

always   often   should (x2)   shouldn't   sometimes

11–18: You are _____ very helpful! You _____ do more tasks. Great job!

6–10: You are _____ helpful. You _____ sometimes do more tasks.

0–5: You are _____ helpful! You _____ do more at home!

5 Write four classroom tasks. Ask a partner and complete.

Tasks   _____'s answers

1 _____   1 _____

2 _____   2 _____

3 _____   3 _____

4 _____   4 _____

Do you empty the bins?

No, I never empty the bins.

6 Look at 5. Complete the sentences about your partner.

_____ should _____ .   _____ shouldn't _____ .

I can talk about rules using should .

Story lab

READING

I will read a story about a holiday adventure.

New friends

1 Read and answer.

1 At first, what does Maryam want to do for the winter holidays?

_____

_____

2 Who is staying in the city?

_____

3 Why does Maryam bump into Oliver?

_____

4 Where is Oliver going?

_____

5 What is the weather like?

_____

6 Why can't Maryam stand up at first?

_____

7 Why does Maryam enjoy her time in the village?

_____

8 Why does Grandma cheer Maryam at the end of the story?

_____

2 Write about the good things that happen to Maryam.

_____

_____

_____

3 Complete the sentences with words from the story.

| Dictionary | Thesaurus | Sentence structures | 🔍 |

1 There are a lot of shops and streets in the _____ .

2 At first, Maryam didn't _____ that the village was fun.

3 If there is nothing to do, you feel _____ .

4 When you move over ice you wear _____ .

5 You can protect your head with a _____ .

6 If you can stand on one leg, you've got good _____ .

4 Read and complete.

always   never   often   sometimes

1   Oliver _____ goes to the village for his holidays.
2   Oliver _____ skates with his friends.
3   Maryam's mum _____ went ice-skating as a child.
4   Oliver is good at skating. He _____ falls over.
5   For the rest of the month, Maryam is _____ bored.

5 Who is your favourite character from the story? Discuss with a partner.

My favourite character is Oliver because he's kind to Maryam.

I agree. Oliver is friendly because he asks Maryam to go ice-skating with his friends.

6 Write a review of a character from the story.

- Choose a character and describe them.
- What's their name and how old are they?
- What do they look like? What are they like: helpful, friendly, kind?
- How does the character feel at the start and end of the story?
- Draw your character doing something that makes them happy.

7 Write your opinion of the story.

- How does Maryam change in the story?
- What do you think of the story?
- Does Maryam enjoy being in the village at the start and end of the story? Why?

| Key |
| 1 = very bad |
| 5 = very good |

My opinion

_____

_____

_____

① ② ③ ④ ⑤

I can   read a story about a holiday adventure.

Experiment lab

I will learn how to balance using my senses.

1 Read and label. Then answer the question.

> footbal   gymnastics   swimming   tennis

1 _____ You use your eyes and your sense of touch for this sport. You need excellent hand-to-eye coordination. You need good balance. A sense of hearing is sometimes important. Players often change direction very quickly.

2 _____ This is a team sport and you use your sense of hearing. You use your eyes and your sense of touch. You need good foot-to-eye coordination. Players don't use their hands. Players run very fast and sometimes they jump.

3 _____ This is an individual sport. Balance isn't important. You don't need your eyes or a sense of hearing. You use your sense of touch. You need strong lungs.

4 _____ You don't need a sense of hearing for this sport, but you need very good balance. You use your eyes and your sense of touch. This is an individual sport. You don't work in a team. You jump and you do cartwheels.

Which senses don't you use in these sports?   _____

2 What skills do you need to do these sports? Look and write.

Key
FE: foot-eye coordination
HE: hand-eye coordination
B: balance
T: team sport
I: individual sport

Tennis _____
Football _____
Ice hockey _____
Basketball _____
Gymnastics _____
Swimming _____
Ice-skating _____

3 Choose your favourite sport and describe the actions.

When I play football, I kick, run and jump.

When I _____ .

4 🎧 029 Listen and complete.

1 A tennis ball can move at _____ kilometres per hour.

2 A football can move at _____ kilometres per hour.

3 A hockey puck can move at _____ kilometres per hour.

4 A table tennis ball can move at _____ kilometres per hour.

5 A volleyball can move at _____ kilometres per hour.

5 Look at 4. Then read and complete.

MATHS ZONE

1 tennis ball _____ hockey puck

2 football _____ volleyball

3 hockey puck _____ volleyball

4 table tennis ball _____ tennis ball

Key

< slower than

> faster than

= the same speed as

EXPERIMENT TIME

Report

1 Describe the experiment and explain your results.

Who was the best at balancing in your group?

What was the most difficult balance for your group?

Which senses help you balance?

_____

_____

2 💬 Read and circle. Then discuss with a partner.
How difficult was the experiment?

1 Following the instructions.   Difficult / OK / Easy

2 Trying the balances.   Difficult / OK / Easy

3 Using the stopwatch.   Difficult / OK / Easy

4 Making the bar chart.   Difficult / OK / Easy

Balancing was easy because I practise yoga.

I know how to balance using my senses.

85

Sharing out tasks

*I will ask and answer using **should**.*

1 🎧 030 **Listen and tick ☑ the tasks.**

TASKS FOR THE DANCE CONTEST

1 invent dance routine ☐
2 find music ☐
3 practise dance routine ☐
4 make costumes ☐
5 practise painting pictures ☐
6 organise journey ☐
7 prepare lunch for journey ☐
8 take costumes ☐

2 Choose and tick ☑ an event. Then find two friends with the same event.

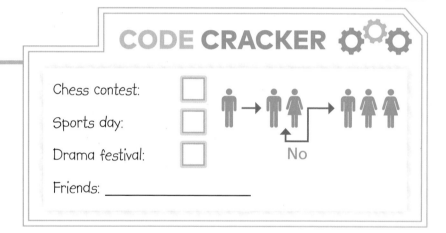

CODE CRACKER ⚙⚙⚙

Chess contest: ☐

Sports day: ☐

Drama festival: ☐

No

Friends: _____

3 Complete the list for your event in 2.

Tasks for _____

1 _____

_____

2 _____

_____

3 _____

_____

4 _____

_____

4 Write an email about who should do which task in 3.

• Look at your list. Who should do the tasks?

• Make suggestions to your friends.

To: _____ and _____ Subject: _____ ✈ 📎 🗐

Hi _____ ,

We should _____ .

_____ .

_____ .

Speak soon, _____

I can ask and answer using should .

Writing lab

I will learn to write a flyer.

FLYERS

1 What is a flyer for? Read and tick ✓ .

1 It gives information. ☐
2 It is funny. ☐
3 It's got a logo. ☐
4 It's got rules. ☐
5 It tells a story. ☐
6 It's got big and small letters. ☐
7 It is for the general public. ☐
8 It is for one person. ☐

2 Write a flyer for a holiday camp.

- Think of a name for the camp and invent a logo.
- Think of two activities you can do at the camp. Why are they fun?
- When is the camp? Where is it? How old are the children?

3 ✎ Write a slogan for the holiday camp and make a collage.

- My camp slogan: _____
- Choose materials for the collage.
- Make the letters in the slogan with the material.
- Glue the letters to a large piece of paper.

A slogan is a phrase or sentence. It sounds good and sends a message.

4 💬 Ask about a partner's flyer and slogan. Take notes.

Name: _____
Name of camp: _____

Skills: _____
Equipment: _____

What skills do I need?

What equipment do I need?

You should be good at running.

You should have shorts and a T-shirt.

I can write a flyer.

Have a club fair

Project report

1 Write a summary of your club.

What type of club is it? _____

When and where are you going to meet? _____

What are the rules? _____

Has it got a logo or a slogan? _____

How many people joined your club? _____

2 Read and answer.

1 Which club logo did you like best? Why?
_____

2 Which club slogan did you like best? Why?
_____

3 Which club item did you like best? Why?
_____

4 Which club had the most interesting activities? Why?
_____

5 Which clubs did you want to join? Why?
_____

3 Read and number for you. Then answer the questions.

| Key | 1 = very easy | 10 = very difficult |

Working in a group. ☐

Finding the favourite type of club. ☐

Thinking of interesting activities. ☐

Inventing the rules. ☐

Inventing the slogan. ☐

Designing the logo. ☐

Making the item. ☐

Explaining the club to my class. ☐

What did you make?
_____

What did you learn?

1 I learnt _____ .

2 _____

3 _____

I can have a club fair.

4 Listen and match. Then answer the question.

- practises at home.
- takes part in competitions.
- Kim always •— • kicks the ball.
- Kim often •— • catches the ball.
- Kim sometimes •— • scores a goal.
- Kim never •— • wears special gloves.
- plays outside.
- plays in a stadium.

Kim

What's Kim's favourite sport? _____

5 Read the letters and complete the replies.

> always   never   should   shouldn't   sometimes

1 I'm often late in the mornings. And I'm tired. What should I do?

From Julia

2 My teacher never puts my pictures on the wall. What should I do?

From Ana

3 Sometimes I can't find my school books. What should I do?

From Juan

Dear _____ ,

You _____ get up earlier and you _____ go to bed late. _____ prepare your school things before you go to bed.

Dear _____ ,

You should _____ be late with your work. Are your pictures tidy? You _____ always be careful with your work. _____ , you can ask for more time.

Dear _____ ,

You _____ put your books away after class. You _____ leave things on the table. _____ give your school books to a friend.

Now go to your Progress Chart on page 4.

3 Checkpoint

UNITS 5 AND 6

1 🎧 032 **Listen and draw lines for Meili. Listen again for Longwei. Then answer the questions.**

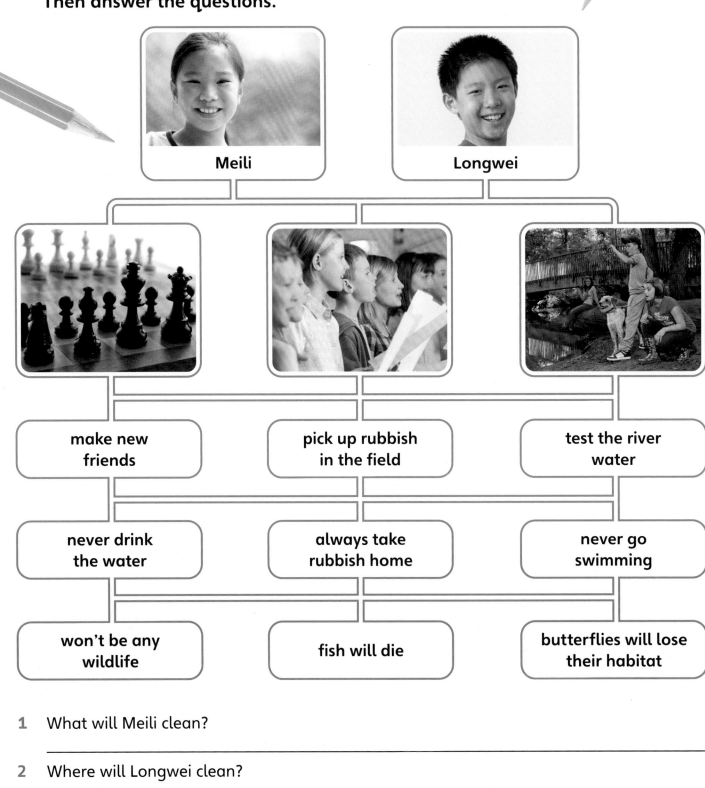

1 What will Meili clean?

_____

2 Where will Longwei clean?

_____

2 Read and write *true*, *false* or *don't know*.

1 Meili and Longwei are in the same neighbourhood club. _____

2 The club they go to always meets on Saturdays. _____

3 They are doing the same thing at the club. _____

4 Meili says people should always take their rubbish home. _____

5 Longwei says people should never drink the water. _____

6 If there is a lot of rubbish in the field, fish will lose their habitat. _____

7 If they clean up around the river, the animals won't lose their habitats. _____

8 If more people join the club, Meili and Longwei won't have anything to do. _____

3 Write a paragraph about a club you want to join and why.

- Think of a type of club.
- If you join the club, what will you do?
- What will you learn?
- How often will you meet?

- What will the rules be?
- What should you do to help?
- What shouldn't you do?

_____

_____

_____

_____

_____

_____

_____

4 Ask a partner about the club they want to join.

What club do you want to join?

Why?

I want to join a choir.

If I join a choir, I'll get good at singing.

The Fathala Wildlife Reserve

1 🔧 **Read and complete. Then listen and check.**

| 12 million | 50 m | 400 km² | 2017 | 3000 years | 8000 km | 300,000 people |

THE GREAT GREEN BELT

The dry lands in the north of Senegal are getting bigger every year. There are fewer trees and grasslands. The loss of habitat is a threat for wildlife and farmers. Around _____ live in this part of Senegal. Many of them are taking part in an international project to stop the growth of the dry lands. It is called the Great Green Belt. More than 10 countries are part of the project. If people in all the countries complete the belt, there will be a living wall of trees from the east to west of Africa. It will be _____ long.

The project started in _____ . In 10 years, people in Senegal planted _____ trees. They saved more than _____ from the dry lands. Many of the trees they planted were baobab trees. The baobab can survive with very little water. It stores water in its long, wide trunk and it hasn't got any leaves for nine months of the year. Baobab trees sometimes live for more than _____ and they can grow up to 30 metres high. The trunk can be wider than _____ . The baobab tree was always an important part of life in the dry areas of Senegal. People eat the fruit and leaves, and they make rope from the bark. Animals eat the leaves and fruit of the baobab tree, and the grass that grows around it, and birds nest in its branches, too. Today it is one of Senegal's national symbols.

2 **Complete the sentences.**

1 If the dry lands get bigger, _____ .

2 If the people plant trees, _____ .

3 If there is more grass, _____ .

3 Read and tick ☑ the correct sentence.

Issa lives in Dakar. It's the capital of Senegal. There are a lot of baobab trees on his street. When he stays with his grandparents, he helps in the new tree plantation. He learns about looking after the trees.

1 Don't water young trees. ☐
2 Don't let animals near young trees. ☐
3 Plant young trees close together. ☐
4 Plant trees that need a lot of water. ☐
5 Don't put fences around young trees. ☐

4 Look at 3. Correct the sentences using should always or should never. Give reasons for your answers.

1 You _____ because _____ .
2 You _____ because _____ .
3 You _____ because _____ .
4 You _____ because _____ .

5 Grow a garden.

Materials: seeds, small plastic pot or tray, soil, water.
1 Choose seeds that grow quickly.
2 Make holes in the bottom of the pot.
3 Fill the pot with soil.
4 Put your seeds 0.5 cm under the soil.
5 Put the pot in a sunny place and water.

6 What tree or plant is a symbol in your country? Explain why it is important.

I live in _____ . Our national symbol is _____ .

It represents _____ .

_____

I know about culture in Senegal.

7 Marvellous medicines

 How can I make a plant fact file?

1 Listen and complete. Then answer.

It is very good for _____ to sit outside in the Sun. Gardens have got a lot of fresh air because the trees and plants give out _____ . Gardens have got _____ and _____ . In the past, _____ used the plants in a hospital garden for _____ .

birds
doctors
flowers
medicine
oxygen
patients

Why are gardens important in a hospital? Discuss with a partner.

2 Read and look at the Braille alphabet. What's the girl's name?

CODE CRACKER

To read, blind people feel words on a page.

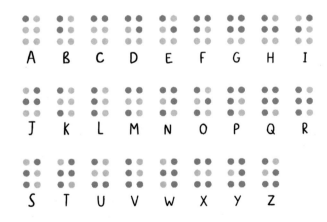

A B C D E F G H I
J K L M N O P Q R
S T U V W X Y Z

3 Make your name label in Braille and stick it on your book.

1 Use a pencil and thick paper. Draw a set of six dots for each letter in your name.

2 Look at the Braille alphabet. Colour the dots for the letters in your name.

3 Use a pencil and push up the coloured dots to make a bump. Don't break the paper.

What's the matter?

I will learn illness and medicine words.

VOCABULARY

1 Read and complete. check-up medicine patients pill temperature thermometer

Doctors have got many different _____ . Everyone should have a _____ with a doctor once a year. If you are hot, the doctor will take your _____ with a _____ . Sometimes the doctor will give you _____ . It is often a _____ .

2 🔊 035 **Listen and number. Then read and answer.**

1 Who needs a bandage? Patient ☐

2 Who needs some cream? Patient ☐

EXTRA VOCABULARY

3 Read and label. Use the words in bold.

John's got a **sling** for his bad arm.
Tim's got a **rash** on his face.

Crutches are good for Mary's bad leg.
Flowers in the spring make Ana **sneeze**.

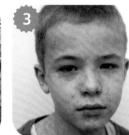
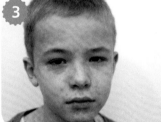

_____ _____ _____ _____

4 Ph **Make words starting with Qu and Tw. The letters in the last group can be used in any order.**

Qu

Tw

a e i

c e s z
o k r y l
n t v i

_____

Language lab

GRAMMAR: TO DO SOMETHING

I will learn to explain why we do something.

1 **Read and complete. Use a word from each box.**

| cover |
| help |
| look at |
| take |

| cut   headache |
| sore back   sore throat |
| teeth   temperature |

1 A dentist uses a small light to _____ .

2 A nurse uses a bandage to _____ .

3 A nurse uses a thermometer to _____ .

4 A doctor uses cream to _____ .

5 A doctor uses pills to _____ .

6 A doctor uses liquid medicine to _____ .

2 036 **What's David going to take to hospital? Listen and tick ✓ .**

a toothbrush ☐   crayons ☐

a computer ☐   a phone ☐

books ☐   a blanket ☐

games ☐

3 **Look at 2. Why is David going to take these things?**

1 He is going to take a _____ to _____ .

2 _____

3 _____

4 _____

4 **What are you going to take to school tomorrow? Tell your partner.**

I'm going to take a pen to school to write notes.

5  **Make a list for staying in hospital. Then ask and answer with a partner and take notes.**

My list	My friend's list
_____	_____
_____	_____
_____	_____
_____	_____

What are you going to take?

I'm going to take a computer.

Why?

To play computer games.

6 Look at 5 and compare the lists.

I'm going to take _____ to _____ .

My friend is going to take _____ to _____ .

I'm _____ .

My friend _____ .

Values Keep healthy.

7 Read and circle.

1 If you've got toothache, you need to visit a dentist / doctor / nurse .

2 You need to visit a dentist twice a year / twice a month / twice a week .

3 You need to brush your teeth once a day / twice a day / three times a day .

4 You need to eat a lot of biscuits / chocolate / vegetables .

5 You need to drink a lot of water / fizzy drinks / fruit juice .

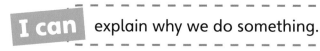 **I can** explain why we do something.

Story lab

READING

I will read a story about a real event.

Cholera outbreak!

1 Read and answer.

1 Who is telling the story?

_____

2 What are the symptoms of cholera?

_____

3 How does cholera spread?

_____

4 What does the doctor do to the pumps? Why?

_____

2 Read and find facts that tell you these things.

1 Cholera is a very dangerous disease.   _____

2 The ill people haven't got water in their houses.   _____

3 There are other areas of London with the disease.   _____

4 The people learn something important.   _____

3 Complete the key with colours. Then colour the pumps and houses.

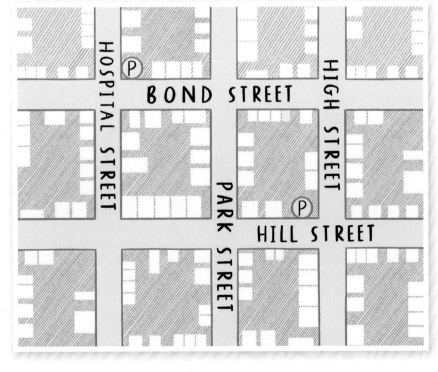

Key

Dirty pump: ◯

Houses with cholera: ▢

Clean pump: ◯

Houses without cholera: ▢

Houses with cholera ...

Hill Street: 10

High Street: 3

Hospital Street: 0

Park Street: 4

Bond Street: 2

4 Read and answer. Then complete the chart and labels.

This cholera outbreak lasted from January to April. There were 600 victims. Half (½) of the victims died in the worst month. In the last month, the number of victims was the same as in the first month. In the second month, a third (⅓) of the victims died.

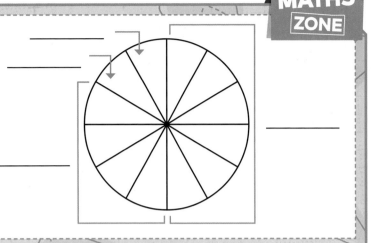

5 Complete the story review.

Title: _____ ★★★★★

Main character: _____ Type of story: _____

Place: _____ Problem: _____

Reason for problem: _____ Solution: _____

6 Write your opinion of the story.

- Where did Dr Snow's patients get water from?
- How did cholera spread?
- How did Dr Snow discover this?
- What did Dr Snow do to stop the cholera outbreak?
- What do you think of the story?

● ● ●

Key	My opinion
1 = very bad	_____
5 = very good	_____
	_____

①   ②   ③   ④   ⑤

I can read a story about a real event.

Experiment lab

SCIENCE: TRACKING GERMS

I will learn how to track germs.

1 💡 Read and label. Then answer the questions.

Cholera discovery   Life   Prizes   Research   Tuberculosis discovery

Robert Koch

1 _____

Robert Koch was a famous German doctor and scientist. He was born in 1843. He was a curious child and taught himself to read at five years old. Koch studied medicine at universities and hospitals in Germany.

2 _____

Koch was the first scientist to link a type of bacteria to an illness. His earliest research was into an illness called anthrax. He set up a laboratory in his home, grew bacteria and used a microscope to study them. This is how he found the bacteria that cause the illness in 1878.

3 _____

Two years later, he found the bacteria that cause tuberculosis. During his research, he discovered the best method to grow bacteria in a laboratory. Scientists grow bacteria in the same way today.

4 _____

In 1883, Koch travelled to Egypt to study an outbreak of cholera. He used a method he had invented to find the cholera bacteria. He studied the way the illness spreads and reached the same conclusions as John Snow. His method to control the spread of the illness is used today.

5 _____

For the rest of his life, he studied different illnesses in Europe, Africa and Asia. He received many prizes for his work. In 1905, he won the Nobel Prize in Medicine. Robert Koch died in Germany in 1910.

1   How was Dr Koch curious when he was a child?

_____

2   What was Dr Koch the first scientist to do?

_____

3   Which diseases did Dr Koch study?

_____

4   Which of his methods do we use today?

_____

2 **Read and complete. There are three extra words. Then mime the actions.**

cream   feet   fingers   hands   soap   twenty   two   water

HOW TO WASH YOUR HANDS

Use _____ and _____ .   Rub your _____ together.

Wash between your _____ .

Wash your hands for _____ seconds.

EXPERIMENT TIME

Report

1 **Describe the experiment and write conclusions.**

Who put chalk on their hands? What did they touch? After the experiment, how many people had chalk on their clothes or on their school things?

What does the experiment explain about bacteria? What did you learn?

_____ and _____ put blue chalk on their hands.

They _____ .

After the experiment, _____ .

_____

2  **Read and circle. Then discuss with a partner. How difficult was the experiment?**

1	Following the instructions.	Difficult / OK / Easy
2	Finding the materials.	Difficult / OK / Easy
3	Finding the chalk marks.	Difficult / OK / Easy
4	Cleaning the classroom after the experiment.	Difficult / OK / Easy
5	Completing the table.	Difficult / OK / Easy

Finding the chalk marks was difficult because I didn't have a light.

I know how to track germs.

101

My head hurts!

COMMUNICATION

I will ask and answer about illnesses.

1  Listen and match.

Mary

Edu

Salma

Simon

Chunhua

My head hurts.

My stomach hurts.

My ear hurts.

My throat hurts.

My back hurts.

2 Read and write D (Doctor) or P (Patient). Then number in order.

_____ Do I need some medicine? ☐

_____ Do your shoulders hurt? ☐

_____ Yes, you do. Here's some cream. ☐

_____ Yes, they do. ☐

_____ What's the matter? ☐

_____ You should sit up straight and take fewer books home. ☐

_____ Yes, there are. ☐

_____ No, I don't. ☐

_____ Are there a lot of books in your backpack? ☐

_____ I've got a terrible backache. ☐

_____ Do you sit with a straight back? ☐

3 Choose a health problem. Then ask and answer with a partner.

backache   earache   headache
sore throat   stomachache

What's the matter, Juan?

My head hurts.

I can ask and answer about illnesses.

Writing lab

DOCTOR'S REPORT

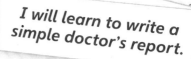

I will learn to write a simple doctor's report.

1  Ask about a partner's report and take notes.

1   Who was your patient? _____

2   When did you do the first visit? _____

3   What was the matter with the patient? _____

4   What medicine did you give? _____

5   What advice did you give? _____

6   When did you do the second visit? _____

7   How was the patient? _____

2 Read and write *advice* or *treatment*.

1   Stay in bed. _____   2   Take this medicine. _____

3   Here are some pills. _____   4   Don't sit under the Sun. _____

5   Drink a lot of water. _____   6   Put this cream on it. _____

7   I'll put a bandage on it. _____   8   Don't go swimming. _____

3 Look at the notes and write a doctor's report.

Name: Maryam Reed

Temperature: 39°C

Problems: earache, sore shoulder

Advice: no swimming, stay in bed

Medicine: ear drops, cream

Sunshine HEALTH CENTRE

Date: _____

Patient: _____

Maryam had _____ °C.

She _____ .

I _____ .

I gave her _____ to _____

_____ .

Signed by _____ .

1 Read and answer about your fact file.

1 How many plants did you research?

_____

2 Which plant did you choose?

_____

3 What part of the plant did people use for medicine?

_____

4 What was the medicine for?

_____

The willow tree

People used willow bark to make medicine that helps people when they've got a high temperature. It makes their temperatures go down to normal. Today, we still use the same plant.

2 Write about the plant fact files.

• How many different plant fact files did your class make? _____

• What was the most popular and the most colourful plant? _____

• Which plant fact file did you find the most interesting? Why?

_____

3 Read and number for you. Then answer the questions.

Key   1 = very easy   10 = very difficult

Finding out about plants. ☐   Finding out about illnesses. ☐

Choosing the plant. ☐   Drawing the plant. ☐

Writing the index card. ☐   Comparing your drawings and information. ☐

Where did you find the information? _____

What did you learn?

1 I learnt _____ .

2 _____

3 _____

I can make a plant fact file.

4 🎧 038 Listen and take notes.

Patient's name: _____ Alex Water _____

Temperature: _____

Problems: _____

Medicine: _____

Advice: _____

5 Read and answer.

1   Why do doctors use thermometers? _____

2   Why do dentists use small lights? _____

3   Why do nurses use bandages? _____

4   Why do doctors use X-rays? _____

5   Why do doctors give medicine to patients? _____

6   Why do doctors give cream to patients? _____

6 Tick ☑ two objects and complete.

backpack ☐   chair ☐   pencil ☐   piece of paper ☐

I can use a _____ to _____ and _____ .

I can use a _____ to _____ and _____ .

7 💬 Ask and answer with a partner.

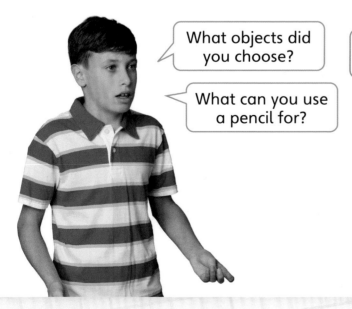

What objects did you choose?

What can you use a pencil for?

I chose a pencil and a chair.

I can use a pencil to write stories and draw pictures.

8 Theme parks

How can I make a model theme park ride?

Robin

Sally

1 🎧 039 Listen and write the names.

1 roller coaster
_____

2 Ferris wheel
_____

3 popcorn
_____

4 ice cream
_____

2 Tick ☑ the theme park activities.

1	building camps ☐	2	going on rides ☐
3	going swimming ☐	4	having some food ☐
5	seeing attractions ☐	6	watching films ☐
7	doing sport ☐	8	watching fireworks ☐

3 Choose two theme park activities from 2. Then find two friends with the same activities.

My favourite theme park activities are _____ and _____ .

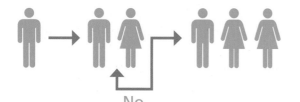

No

CODE CRACKER

What are your two favourite activities?

I like going on rides and watching fireworks.

Me, too!

Rides!

VOCABULARY

I will learn theme park words.

1 Read and complete.

> candyfloss   crisps   Ferris wheel   hot dog
> queueing   roller coaster   scared   taking a seat

1   Longwei is _____ to go on his favourite ride. It goes around and around in a circle. What is it? _____

2   Melek's favourite ride is about to start. She's _____ . It goes up and down, and around and around. What is it? _____

3   Edu is sitting in his favourite ride. He's screaming because he's _____ .

4   Longwei's favourite snack is sweet and it's often pink. What is it? _____

5   Melek's favourite snack is brown and comes in bread. What is it? _____

6   Edu's favourite snack is in a plastic bag. What is it? _____

EXTRA VOCABULARY

2 Read and label. Use the words in bold.

A **merry-go-round** goes around and around.
It's often got model animals to sit on.

Edu is queueing in a long queue. He's very **bored**.

A **water slide** goes up very high and then down again into water.

Melek is watching people making **doughnuts** at the theme park.

1 _____   2 _____

3 _____   4 _____

3 Ph Find words with the same sound. Circle the letters in red or green.

> fa(ce)   gi(a)nt

July   pencil   June   gloves   dance   December   gym
exciting   girl   ice   jelly

Language lab

GRAMMAR: PAST, PRESENT AND FUTURE

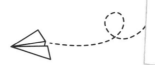

I will learn to compare the past, present and future.

1 Read and complete.

in the afternoon   in the evening   in the morning

Theme park information

Opening time: 9:00 _____

Closing time: 8:00 _____

First ride: 10:00 _____

Last ride: 7:00 _____

Gymnastic displays:

- 11:00–12:00 _____
- 4:00–5:00 _____
- 6:00–7:00 _____
- Exhibition rooms closed: 12:00–3:00 _____
- The café is open all day.
- Lunch hours: 12:00–2:00 _____

2 Look at **1**. Complete the plan.

You can go on three rides. The rides last for 30 minutes. You will queue for 10 minutes for all the rides, attractions and snacks. You want to see the gymnastic display and go to the exhibition. You are going to have lunch. You can have a snack in the morning or afternoon.

PLAN FOR THE THEME PARK

Arrive at _____

Snack at _____

Lunch at _____

Gymnastics display at _____

Leave at _____

First ride: _____ at _____

Second ride: _____ at _____

Exhibition at _____

Third ride: _____ at _____

3 Look at 2. Read and answer.

It's 11 o'clock.

1 What are you doing now?

_____

2 What did you do before?

_____

3 What will you do next?

_____

It's three o'clock.

4 What are you doing now?

_____

5 What did you do before?

_____

6 What will you do next?

_____

4 Choose a time. Ask a partner and take notes.   10:00   1:00   4:00

_____'s plans

It's _____ o'clock.

Before: _____

At: _____

After: _____

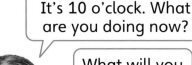 It's 10 o'clock. What are you doing now?

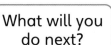 What will you do next?

What did you do before?

5 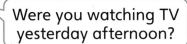 Look at 2 and 4. Compare your day with your partner's.

- What did you do before?
- Did your partner do the same thing?
- What will you do next?
- Will your partner do the same thing?

_____

_____

_____

_____

6 Make a time catcher. Play *Choose my action.*

1 Use a square piece of paper and fold the corners to the centre.

2 Turn the paper over and write actions in each triangle.

3 Then fold the corners to the centre again.

4 Turn the paper over again and write a time and day in each triangle.

5 Fold it in half and write four different colours on the squares.

Were you watching TV yesterday afternoon?

No, I wasn't.

 I can compare the past, present and future.

Story lab

READING

I will read a story about a theme park adventure.

Who's lost?

1 **Read and circle T (True) or F (False).**

1   Meili sees her friend on the roller coaster.   T / F
2   Uncle Bohai bought popcorn for Yong.   T / F
3   The people in the café go to see a gymnastics display.   T / F
4   Meili sees Yong at the gymnastics display.   T / F
5   Yong sees Meili riding the dodgems.   T / F
6   Yong finds Meili in the information office.   T / F

2 **Find words in the story that mean ...**

1   ... said something in a very loud voice. _____
2   ... a message for the public. _____
3   ... a performance for the public. _____
4   ... the opposite of full. _____
5   ... very bad. _____
6   ... not knowing where something or someone is. _____

3 **Draw Yong's route.**

4 **Look at 3. Write how Yong feels at each place.**

excited   happy   scared   worried

Yong feels _____ .
Yong _____ .
Yong _____ .
_____
_____
_____
_____

5 Write a paragraph about Yong's day at the theme park.

What does Yong do?

Where does he go?

Who is he with and what happens?

Where does he find his sister?

6 Complete the story review.

Title: _____ ★★★★★

Main characters: _____

Place: _____

Events: _____

Solution: _____

Type of story: _____

Problem: _____

Reason for problem: _____

7 Write your opinion of the story.

- Do you think Yong enjoys his visit to the theme park? Why?
- Do you think Bohai is a good uncle? Why?
- Do you like the story? Why?
- What do you think of the story?

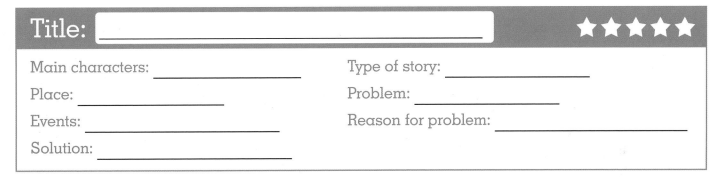

Key

1 = very bad
5 = very good

My opinion

_____

_____

_____

① ② ③ ④ ⑤

 read a story about a theme park adventure.

Experiment lab

SCIENCE: FORCES OF MOTION

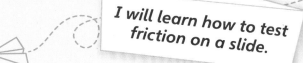

I will learn how to test friction on a slide.

1 Read, choose and write.   centrifugal force   friction   gravity   momentum

1 All moving objects have got this. We calculate this by measuring the weight and speed of the object. This is greater for a heavy object than a lighter one. It is also greater for a fast-moving object than a slower one.
What is this? _____

2 This pulls objects toward the Earth. This is how the Earth spins around the Sun. This is the same for all objects.
What is this? _____

3 When a moving object rubs against a surface it makes this. It slows down a moving object. We can reduce this with a smooth, shiny surface.
What is this? _____

4 When an object is in a spinning machine, this pushes it away from the centre. The object travels in a straight line to the sides. The wall of the machine stops the movement of the object. What is this? _____

2 Read and answer.

1 A car and a bike are travelling at the same speed. Which one's got greater momentum?

_____

2 What force makes the Moon spin around the Earth?

_____

3 Why do we fall over if we walk on ice?

_____

3 Read, choose and write.   dodgems   Ferris wheel   spinner

1 Friction is very important for this ride. It doesn't use centrifugal forces. _____

2 Friction isn't very important for this ride. It works with gravity and momentum. _____

3 Friction isn't very important for this ride. It works with centrifugal forces. _____

4 Cross ☒ the steps that are not needed. Then number in order.

When we do a scientific experiment, we follow the scientific method.
There are six steps in the scientific method.

a ☐ Analyse the data.

b ☐ Suggest an answer.

c ☐ Do an experiment to collect data.

d ☐ Share your results.

e ☐ Change the data.

f ☐ Reach a conclusion.

g ☐ Draw a picture.

h ☐ Ask a question.

EXPERIMENT TIME

Report

1 Write your results and work out the average times.

MATHS ZONE

Look at the results when the slide has got aluminium foil.

Add up the results for each roll. Divide the result by 3.

Repeat the steps with sugar and glue.

	Aluminium foil:	Sugar and glue:
Me	Roll 1: _____	Roll 1: _____
	Roll 2: _____	Roll 2: _____
	Roll 3: _____	Roll 3: _____
Total:	_____	_____
Average:	_____ / 3 = _____	_____ / 3 = _____

2 Describe the experiment and write conclusions.

When does the marble go faster and slower?   Which surface has got more or less friction?

_____

_____

3 Read and circle. Then discuss. How difficult was the experiment?

1 Following the instructions.   Difficult / OK / Easy

2 Making the slide.   Difficult / OK / Easy

3 Covering the slide with sugar and glue.   Difficult / OK / Easy

Covering the slide with glue and sugar was difficult.

I know how to test friction on a slide.

Expressing feelings

COMMUNICATION

I will express my feelings.

1  Listen and tick ☑.

		David	Anna	Jack	Jane
Scared of	... getting lost				
	... fast rides				
Interested in	... gymnastics display				
	... exhibitions				
Worried about	... the long queues				
	... getting hot				
Excited about	... riding the Ferris wheel				
	... being with friends				

2 Imagine you will visit a theme park. Write about your feelings.

- What are you excited about?
- What are you interested in?
- What are you scared of?
- What are you worried about?

 Face fears.

3 Read and answer. Then discuss with a partner.

Face your fears

1 Are you scared of getting lost?
a always   b sometimes   c never

2 Are you scared of storms?
a always   b sometimes   c never

3 Are you worried about forgetting your homework?
a always   b sometimes   c never

4 Are you worried about being late for school?
a always   b sometimes   c never

Points: a = 5, b = 3, c = 0

I'm sometimes scared of the dark. Are you?

Yes! I'm always scared of the dark.

I'm not, but I'm sometimes scared of getting lost.

I can express my feelings.

Writing lab

LOST PROPERTY FORM

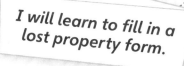

I will learn to fill in a lost property form.

1 Ask about a partner's lost property. Take notes.

Name: _____   Lost object: _____

Date: _____   Time of day: _____

Last place: _____

2 Read and sort. Then add more words.

backpack   dodgems   café
having lunch   phone
queueing   scarf   toilets
roller coaster

Objects	Places	Actions

3 Read and complete with words from 2.

Mary and Edu Gomez went to a Space theme park on Saturday. Mary had a _____ and Edu had a _____ . In the morning, they went on the _____ and the _____ . Then they went to the _____ . When they were _____ , Edu saw he didn't have his _____ .

Mary

Edu

4 Complete the form. Use information from 3 and your imagination.

SPACE WORLD

Name: _____   Address: _____

Telephone number: _____   Lost object: _____

Date: _____   Time of day: _____

Last place you had the object: _____

Other notes: _____

I can fill in a lost property form.

Make a model theme park ride

Project report

1 Read and complete about your theme park.

Name of theme park: _____

Type of rides: _____

My ride: _____

Materials for my ride: _____

Other features: _____

2 Write about your theme park.

- Who did you work with?
- How did you make it?
- What did the theme park look like?

- What ride did you make?
- Were you interested in the project? Why?

_____

_____

_____

_____

3 Read and number for you.

Finding out about theme parks. ☐

Choosing a ride to make. ☐

Making the ride. ☐

Arranging all the rides on the board. ☐

Guessing the other rides. ☐

Key   1 = very easy   10 = very difficult

Working with your partner. ☐

Finding the materials. ☐

Decorating the ride. ☐

Explaining how I made my ride. ☐

What did you learn?

1   I learnt _____ .

2   _____

3   _____

I can make a model theme park ride.

4 Read, listen and answer.

Grace

Cecil

a dodgems   b snack
c gymnastics display   d lunch
e Ferris wheel   f exhibition
g roller coaster

1 What did Grace do before? ☐ ☐ ☐

2 What is she doing now? ☐

3 What will she do? ☐

4 What did Cecile do before? ☐ ☐ ☐

5 What is he doing now? ☐

6 What will he do? ☐

5 Look at 4 and answer.

1 What did Grace do before the snack?

_____

2 What did she do after the snack?

_____

3 What will she do after lunch?

_____

4 What did Cecil do before the exhibition?

_____

5 What did he do after the exhibition?

_____

6 What will he do after the dodgems?

_____

6 Look at 4. Play *Guess the path*.

What are you doing now?

What did you do before?

What will you do next?

4 Checkpoint

UNITS 7 AND 8

1 🎧 042 **Listen and draw lines for Tim. Listen again for Alice. Then answer the questions.**

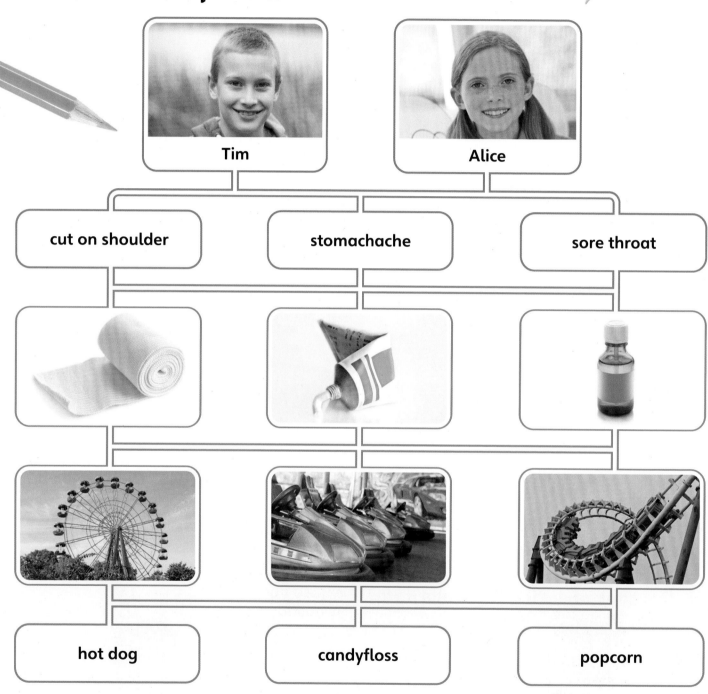

Tim

Alice

cut on shoulder

stomachache

sore throat

hot dog

candyfloss

popcorn

1   Why has Tim got a stomachache?

_____

2   How did Alice hurt her shoulder?

_____

2 Read and write *true*, *false* or *don't know*.

1   Tim needs some medicine for his stomachache.   _____

2   Alice needs some cream for her shoulder.   _____

3   Tim was scared of the roller coaster.   _____

4   Alice went on the Ferris wheel.   _____

5   Tim and Alice ate popcorn at the theme park.   _____

6   Tim ate a lot of candyfloss at the theme park.   _____

7   Alice and Tim go to school together.   _____

8   Tim will see the doctor before Alice.   _____

3 Write a paragraph about your feelings and interests.

Are you excited about something in the future?

What are you excited about?

What are you interested in at school?

What are you scared of? Why?

What are you worried about? Why?

_____

_____

_____

_____

4 Ask a partner about their feelings and interests.

What are you excited about?

I'm excited about my holiday.

Why?

Because I'll go to the beach.

Fairgrounds and The Goose Fair

CULTURE

1 **Read and write a title for each paragraph.**

> The UK is made up of England, Scotland, Wales and Northern Ireland.

1 _____ ☆

800 years ago, fairs were very different from the fairs today. They had a serious side. Some people went to fairs to find work or to sell goods. Other people went to buy goods. People could buy medicines at a fair and they could see a dentist. People also went to fairs to have fun. Travelling actors, musicians, jugglers, strongmen and unusual animals were some of the early fair attractions.

2 _____ ☆ ☆ ☆

Then, about 150 years ago, a new type of fair attraction appeared at a fair in England. It was a moving merry-go-round. It moved using a new invention, steam power. During the following years, travelling show people used new technology to invent many different rides.

3 _____ ☆

Travelling show people helped to introduce important inventions to people who lived outside the big cities. Some people saw their first motorcar or their first film at a fair. Shows using electricity or X-rays were also popular.

4 _____ ☆ ☆ ☆

Travelling show people invented many of our favourite fair rides like dodgems or the Ferris wheel. There are problems for fairs in the future. Fair rides use a lot of fuel and they produce air pollution. Also, there isn't a lot of space in many towns for a fair. But fairs are still popular for people of all ages in England. In the future, travelling show people will invent new, ecological fair rides.

2 **Find words in the text that mean ...**

1   ... a person who throws and catches balls in the air. _____

2   ... a fair ride that goes around in a circle. _____

3   ... water in its form as a gas. _____

4   ... to show for the first time. _____

5   ... new ways of using new technology. _____

6   ... a liquid to make engines move. _____

3 Read and answer.

Ella's family has got a long history working at the fairs. Her great-grandfather, Bob, was the first member of the family to work as a travelling showman. Ella still visits the same fairs as her great-grandfather. But her way of life is very different. Bob didn't have a caravan. He was a photographer and he took his equipment on trains. Sometimes his family didn't travel with him. Ella's grandfather bought the first family caravan. It was very small, and it didn't have a bathroom or heating. In the winter, they stayed in a family house. Ella lives in the caravan all year long. It's as comfortable as a house.

A generation is about 25 years and Ella is 9.

1   When was her great-grandfather born?

_____

2   Why did he travel by train?

_____

3   When was her grandfather born?

_____

4   What was the problem with his caravan?

_____

5   Why didn't he spend all year in the caravan?

_____

6   Where does Ella live in the winter?

_____

4  Make a blueprint to show the inside of a caravan.

1   Imagine the inside of a caravan from above.
2   Use a piece of graph paper and draw a long rectangle for the outline.
3   Draw the rooms and furniture from above.
4   You need a kitchen, a bathroom, a living room and space for four beds.
5   Label any special features.

5 Write a paragraph about a theme park or fair in your country.

• What's the name of the theme park or fair? Where is it?
• What rides and attractions has it got?

_____

_____

_____

Unit 1

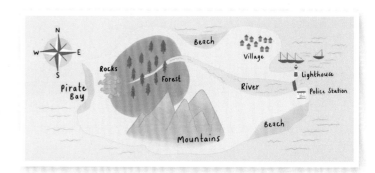

TRAVEL BROCHURE

- Choose a place for an adventure camp.
- Think of a name and mark it on the map.
- Invent different adventures.
- Complete a list of equipment.

COME TO _____ CAMP

We've got a lot of adventures around the island!

Adventure 1:

_____

Adventure 2:

_____

Adventure 3:

_____

Useful equipment:

_____

Unit 2

DIARY ENTRY

- Imagine you live in Aztec times.
- Imagine an ordinary day in your life.
- What did you do? Who did you see? Where did you go?
- Write about your day.

My Diary

Name: _____   Date: _____

Today, I _____

_____

_____

_____

Unit 3

SHAPE POEM

- Invent a name for your space city.
- Write it at the top or sides of your city. You can write it a lot of times.
- Choose a topic for each level.

animals   food   homes   offices   play   shops   vegetable garden   waste

- Draw around each level with a different colour.
- Think of words for each level and write them in the space.
- You can use BIG or small letters.
- You can decorate the letters and the words.

Unit 4

DIALOGUE WRITING

- Look at your story.
- Imagine a conversation between the two characters.
- How does the conversation start?
- Do the characters know each other?
- Choose expressions.

What's new? ☐	Hi! ☐	It's nice to see you. ☐	Hello! What's your name? ☐	Hello! It's nice to meet you. ☐

Choose a theme for the conversation. family future plans past events the weather

- Use two expressions to start the conversation.
- Think of two questions about the theme.
- Think of answers for the questions.
- Write a conversation between the characters.
- Use your sock puppets and role-play the conversation.
- Say goodbye at the end of the conversation.

Hello! What's your name?

Are you going to go to the river?

Max. It's nice to meet you.

Yes, I am.

'_____ !' the _____ said.

'_____ ', the _____ said.

'_____ ?'

the _____ asked.

'_____ ',

the _____ answered.

'_____ ?'

the _____ asked.

'_____ ',

the _____ answered.

'_____ ', the _____ said.

'_____ ', the _____ said.

Unit 5

FACT FILE

- Imagine you work at a wildlife observation centre and choose a name.

- Where in the world is the wildlife centre?

- Research an endangered animal that lives near the place. Draw or find a picture of the animal.

- What does the animal look like? What does the animal eat?

- Are there more or fewer animals than ten years ago? What threats are there to the animal?

_____ Wildlife Centre

Place: Habitat:

Animal Fact File

Name of animal:

Description:

What does it eat?

Number of animals:

Threats:

Unit 6

SPORT REPORT

- Imagine you were at a sport event for a school team. What sport was it? Where was the event?

- Imagine an important moment in the event.

- What happened? When did it happen? Why did it happen? What did people say?

- Write about the event for the school magazine. Draw a picture.

🛡 *Champions School Magazine*

_____

_____

_____

_____

_____

Unit 7

BIOGRAPHY

- Choose a famous doctor.
- Research and find answers to the questions:

  1   Where was the doctor born?   2   Where did the doctor live?

  3   What special area did the doctor study?   4   What experiments did the doctor do?

  5   What did the doctor discover?   6   Why was the discovery important?

- Think of a title and write four paragraphs: Life, Research, Discovery, Conclusion.
- Find and add a picture or illustration to the biography.

FAMOUS DOCTORS FROM HISTORY

Insert photo

_____

LIFE

_____
_____
_____
_____

RESEARCH

_____
_____
_____
_____

DISCOVERY

_____
_____
_____

CONCLUSION

_____
_____
_____
_____

Unit 8

PRESENTATION

- Imagine you are starting a new school next year.
- Write a presentation about yourself.
- Write four paragraphs:
  1 Personal information: your name, age, address
  2 Favourite activities: school subjects, after-school clubs, weekend activities
  3 Feelings: scared of …, interested in …, worried about …, excited about …
  4 Hopes for the future: your new school, your future job, in 10 years …
- Include a picture of yourself.

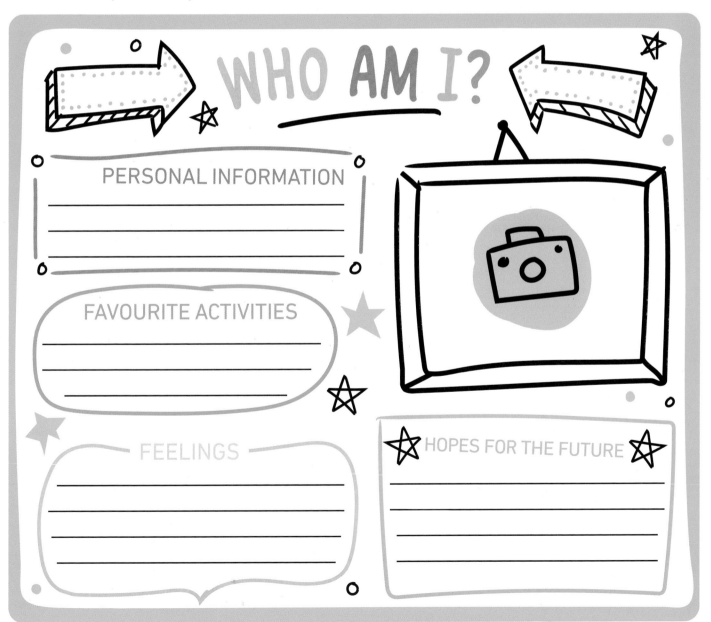

WHO AM I?

PERSONAL INFORMATION

FAVOURITE ACTIVITIES

FEELINGS

HOPES FOR THE FUTURE

Pearson Education Limited
KAO TWO
KAO Park
Hockham Way
Harlow, Essex
CM17 9SR
England

and Associated Companies throughout the world.

english.com/englishcode

First published 2021
Eighth impression 2023

ISBN: 978-1-292-32280-3

Set in Heinemann Roman 12 pt
Printed in Slovakia by Neografia

Acknowledgements

The publishers and author(s) would like to thank the following people and institutions for their feedback and comments during the development of the material:

Argentina

Maria Belen Gonzalez Milbrandt (Director Colegio Sol De Funes), Alejandra Garre (Coordinator Colegio San Patricio), Patricia Bettucci (Teacher Colegio Verbo Encarnado), Colegio Los Arroyos (Coordinator Luciana Pittondo), Instituto Stella Maris (Coordinator Ana Maria Ferrari), Gabriela Dichiara (Coordinator Nivel Pre-Primario En Escuela Normal N° 1 Dr Nicolas Avellaneda), Alejandra Ferreyra & Maria Elena Casals (Profesor Escuela Normal N° 1 Dr Nicolas Avellaneda), Maria Julia Occhi (Primary Director Colegio San Bartolomé Sede Fisherton), Gisele Manzur (English Director- Colegio Educativo Latinoamericano), Griselda Rodriguez (Ex-Directora de Instituto IATEL), Cultural Inglesa de Santa Fe (Olga Poloni y Silvia Cantero), Escuela Primaria de la Universidad Nacional del Litoral (Santa Fe) (Ricardo Noval, Natalia Mártirez y Romina Papini), Colegio La Salle Jobson Santa Fe (Santa Fe) (Miriam Ibañez), Colegio de la Inmaculada Concepción (Santa Fe) (Gabriela Guglielminetti), Colegios Niño Jesús y San Ezequiel Moreno (Santa Fe) (Ivana Serrano), Advice Prep School (Santa Fe) (Virginia Berutti), Centro de Enseñanza de Inglés Mariana G. Puygros (Santa Fe). Focus Group Participants: Alejandra Aguirre (Coordinator Colegio Español), Alicia Ercole (Director Instituto CILEL (Casilda)), Marianella Robledo (Coordinator Insituto CILEL (Casilda)), Viviana Valenti (Director Instituto Let's Go), Natalia Berg (Prof. Colegio de La Paz (San Nicolás)).

Turkey

Ugur Okullari, Isik Okullari, Doğa Koleji, Fenerbahce Koleji, Arı Okullari, Maya Okullari, Yükselen Koleji, Pinar Koleji, Yeşilköy Okullari, Final Okullari, Vizyon Koleji

Image Credits:

123RF.com: 16, Alexandre Zveiger 47, Anton Starikov 41, belchonock 60, bilanol 95, Cathy Yeulet 102, 105, Chris Rose 34, David Steele 67, feverpitched 96, grafner 84, Hongqi Zhang 79, Jacek Chabraszewski 79, Kleber Cordeiro Costa 49, Leah-Anne Thompson 95, linux87 23, Vereshchagin Dmitry 41, vladimiroquai 16; **Alamy Images:** tbkmedia.de 37; **Getty Images:** angie7 118, Elke Van de Velde 61, Eva Mårtensson 36, Fabrice Lerouge 118, Feifei Cui-Paoluzzo 106, George Doyle 8, GlobalStock 45, Grafissimo 22, Inti St Clair 30, JBryson 27, Jose Luis Pelaez Inc 30, 30, 49, 49, Juanmonino 61, 62, Khosrork 50, Laura Olivas 62, Moncherie 10, Monkey Business Images 34, monkeybusinessimages 117, Oliver Rossi 21, PeopleImages 106, Rob Lewine 21, Sean Justice 90, Simon Winnall 61, uschools 6, Vostok 47; **Pearson Education Asia Ltd:** Tsz-shan Kwok 41; **Pearson Education Ltd:** Jon Barlow 6, 7, 10, 13, 17, 18, 21, 25, 29, 33, 35, 38, 41, 46, 47, 49, 50, 53, 57, 58, 59, 61, 63, 69, 73, 74, 77, 81, 83, 85, 87, 90, 91, 97, 101, 102, 105, 106, 108, 117, 119, Miguel Dominguez Muñoz 47, Rob Judges 117; **Shutterstock.com:** 90, 97011 11, A_Belov 31, a_v_d 118, Africa Studio 11, 118, Agnieszka Bacal 67, Alinute Silzeviciute 79, Ana del Castillo 107, Anna Om 102, 115, Anton_Ivanov 92, Blue Iris 66, BlueOrange Studio 62, Boule 76, Budimir Jevtic 95, Carlos E. Santa Maria 56, Catalin Petolea 93, chinasong 47, Christophe Testi 62, Dan Logan 16, Darrin Henry 80, David Acosta Allely 67, David Orcea 23, DK Arts 16, dmitro2009 106, Eoghan McNally 31, Evgeny Bakharev 121, FabrikaSimf 11, Feng Yu 108, fototehnik 22, Grigorita Ko 66, Gualberto Becerra 65, gvictoria 102, hd connelly 118, Iakov Filimonov 79, Jacek Chabraszewski 106, james_stone76 67, Janis

Smits 107, Jaya Tri Hartono 72, Jixin YU 16, JohnKwan 31, Kenishirotie 78, Kinga 49, 102, Kletr 118, krishnaobhasa 107, kviktor 118, Lia Koltyrina 62, Lukas Gojda 2, 34, 62, 90, 118, Lyakhova Evgeniya 95, Maciek A 34, Madlen 41, mahakaal 23, Mahathir Mohd Yasin 101, mamahoohooba 6, Martin Charles Hatch 118, Microstock Man 106, Morphart Creation 100, Normana Karia 11, Palmer Kane LLC 21, 30, 102, 115, Panwasin seemala 68, Robbi 20, 32, 48, 76, Robert Ford 107, 120, Sean Pavone 16, SkillUp 20-21, 32-33, 36, 37, 48-49, 60-61, 64, 65, 73, 74, 76-77, 88-89, 92, 93, 101, 104-105, 113, 116-117, 120, 121, SpeedKingz 90, Steve Silver Smith 90, STILLFX 64, Sundry Photography 23, SurangaSL 36, Syda Productions 48, Teresa Kasprzycka 89, ThunderWaffle 72, Tracy Whiteside 21, Tristan Tan 76, Tushchakorn 45, Vadim Sadovski 38, Vilant 34, wavebreakmedia 94, wildestanimal 66, wolfness72 93, Wong Yu Liang 96, Wynian 93, Zurijeta 34, 61

All other images © Pearson Education

Video screenshots:
Jungle Creative

Illustrated by:
Gabriele Antonini/Lemonade Illustration Agency, pp.11, 19, 23, 24, 33, 72, 95, 124; Julia Castaño/The Bright Agency, p.3; Genie Espinosa/Bright Agency, pp.110 (middle); Chloe Evans/Beehive Illustration, pp.12, 14, 45, 53, 98, 110 (bottom), 122; Philip Hailstone/Beehive Illustration, pp.20, 37, 48, 50, 65, 71, 104; Joshua Heinsz/Bright Agency, p.15; Jordan Kincaid/ Beehive Illustration, pp.42 (top), 43 (middle); Gustavo Mazali/Beehive Illustration, p.9; Carl Morris/Beehive Illustration, pp.54-55; Isabel Muñoz/ Bright Agency, p.82; Davide Ortu/Beehive Illustration, p.70; Lucy Semple/ Bright Agency, p.46; Valerie Sindelar/Bright Agency, pp.51, 116; Erin Taylor/ Bright Agency, pp.26-27; Diego Vaisberg/Advocate Art, pp.6, 16, 32, 39, 42 (middle), 123; Joseph Wilkins/Beehive illustration, pp.4-5.

Cover Image: Front: **Pearson Education Ltd:** Jon Barlow